Level 1

openMind

Mickey Rogers • Joanne Taylore-Knowles • Steve Taylore-Knowles

Concept development: Mariela Gil Vierma

MACMILLAN

Contents

Unit	Grammar	Vocabulary	Pronunciation
Unit 1	***be*—statements and *yes/no* questions** ***be*—information questions** Subject pronouns *in* + month *on* + date *at* + time *What/Where/When/How old ...?*	**Useful questions** **Ordinal numbers** Personal information School subjects Interests Countries Months of the year Numbers	**SOUNDS:** the alphabet
Unit 2	**Articles *an* and *a*** **Possessive nouns—'s and s'** *be*—information questions with *Who* *What do you do?* *What does he/she do?*	**Occupations** **Family members** Adjectives for describing jobs Adjectives for describing employees	**WORDS:** two-syllable nouns
Unit 3	**Simple present—statements and *yes/no* questions** **Simple present—information questions** Third person singular spelling rules *be* + adjective	**Free time activities** **Personality adjectives** *like, love, hate, prefer* Everyday activities Types of movie Skills (*draw, paint, etc.*)	**SOUNDS:** third person -*s*
Unit 4	**Frequency adverbs** **Clauses with *until, before, after*** *How often ...?* *What time is it?* *What time do you ...?*	**Telling time** **Prepositions of time** Routine and free time activities Time expressions (*in the morning, every day*, etc.) Days of the week	**WORDS:** days of the week
Unit 5	***there is/there are* with *some, any, several, a lot, many*** ***should*** Imperative for directions *How do I get to (the) ...?* *How do I get there?*	**Places and attractions in a city** **Locations and directions** Adjectives for describing places *probably/definitely*	**WORDS:** compound nouns
Unit 6	**Present progressive** **Present progressive vs. simple present** Spelling rules for *–ing* verbs Verbs not used in the progressive form: *like, know, want, need*	**Lifestyle adjectives** **A green lifestyle** Time expressions (*right now, these days*, etc.)	**WORDS:** stressed verbs

Contents

	Grammar	Vocabulary	Pronunciation
Unit 7	*can/can't*—ability *can/can't* with adverbs of manner Spelling rules for forming regular adverbs irregular adverbs	Personality adjectives Talents and abilities Adverbs of manner *really, very* Languages Sports	**SOUNDS:** *can/can't*
Unit 8	*this, that, these, those* Comparative adjectives Singular and plural nouns *It's/They're* + adj *Can I ...?* *Would you like to ...?* *How much is ...?*	Clothes Adjectives for describing gadgets Things you buy in stores Adjectives for describing clothes Currencies Frequency expressions Events	**SENTENCE RHYTHM:** emphasis with *this, that, these, those*
Unit 9	Count and noncount nouns with *some, any* Verb phrases *Let's ...* *How about ...?*	Food Ordering in a restaurant Meals of the day Phone language Types of restaurants Different ways of cooking food (*baked, fried,* etc.)	**SENTENCE RHYTHM:** weak *to*
Unit 10	Simple past—affirmative statements Simple past—questions and negative statements Spelling rules for simple past regular verbs Regular and irregular verbs	Adjectives with *-ed* and *-ing* Memorable experiences Past time expressions Adjectives for describing trips and experiences Sequencing words	**WORDS:** *-ed* endings
Unit 11	Simple past with *when* clauses Object pronouns Regular and irregular verbs	Life events Historical events Occupations	**SENTENCE RHYTHM:** object pronouns
Unit 12	Present progressive as future *going to* *Why don't we/you...?*	Phrases with *go* *start/stop* + gerund Time expressions (*tomorrow, next month,* etc.) Weekend plans Resolutions Activities to improve your English	**WORDS:** *-ing* verbs with *-y*

In openMind 1 you will ...

Unit 1
- learn how to ask classroom questions.
- introduce yourself and respond to introductions.
- ask for and give personal information.
- practice spelling and recording names.
- use phrases to ask for help.

Unit 2
- talk about the occupations of your family members.
- talk about the occupations of famous people.
- say who your family members are.
- talk about important aspects of careers.

Unit 3
- say which hobbies you like and dislike.
- talk about your free time preferences.
- describe the personality of a friend or family member.

Unit 4
- talk about the times and days when you do things.
- describe your own routines and other people's routines.
- read, write, and speak about people who do not have typical lives.
- explain the sequence of events in your life.

Unit 5
- describe tourist attractions to a visitor to your town.
- describe and give your opinion on your neighborhood.
- ask for and give advice on places to visit in your town.
- request and give directions and check you understand them.

Unit 6
- explore different lifestyles and compare them to yours.
- write and speak about life right now and in general.
- talk about how "green" you are.

Unit 7
- explain your own talents and find out those of other people.
- talk about your positive qualities and write about somebody else's.
- discuss your own talents and those of a talented individual.
- find out the abilities of your classmates.

Unit 8
- give opinions on clothes and talk about shopping.
- listen to prices and give opinions on how much things cost.
- make comparisons between gadgets and give opinions.

Unit 9
- discuss attitudes to food and personal preferences.
- practice accepting and refusing invitations for various situations.
- act out a restaurant scene.
- give opinions on different kinds of restaurants and choose where to go.
- plan different meal situations (a special occasion, eating out) and make menus.

Unit 10
- talk about a short trip or vacation.
- talk about different positive experiences.
- ask and answer questions about past events.
- talk about memorable experiences.

Unit 11
- ask for and give biographical information.
- talk about historical events.
- talk about your childhood.

Unit 12
- discuss plans and arrangements.
- talk about future changes in your life.
- make a plan for and discuss how to improve your English.

English around the World

A Underline any English words that you understand in the ads below.

B What other ads do you know with English words in them?

1 **Language use:** completing an online registration

A Look at this web page. Answer the question. What is MyFriends?

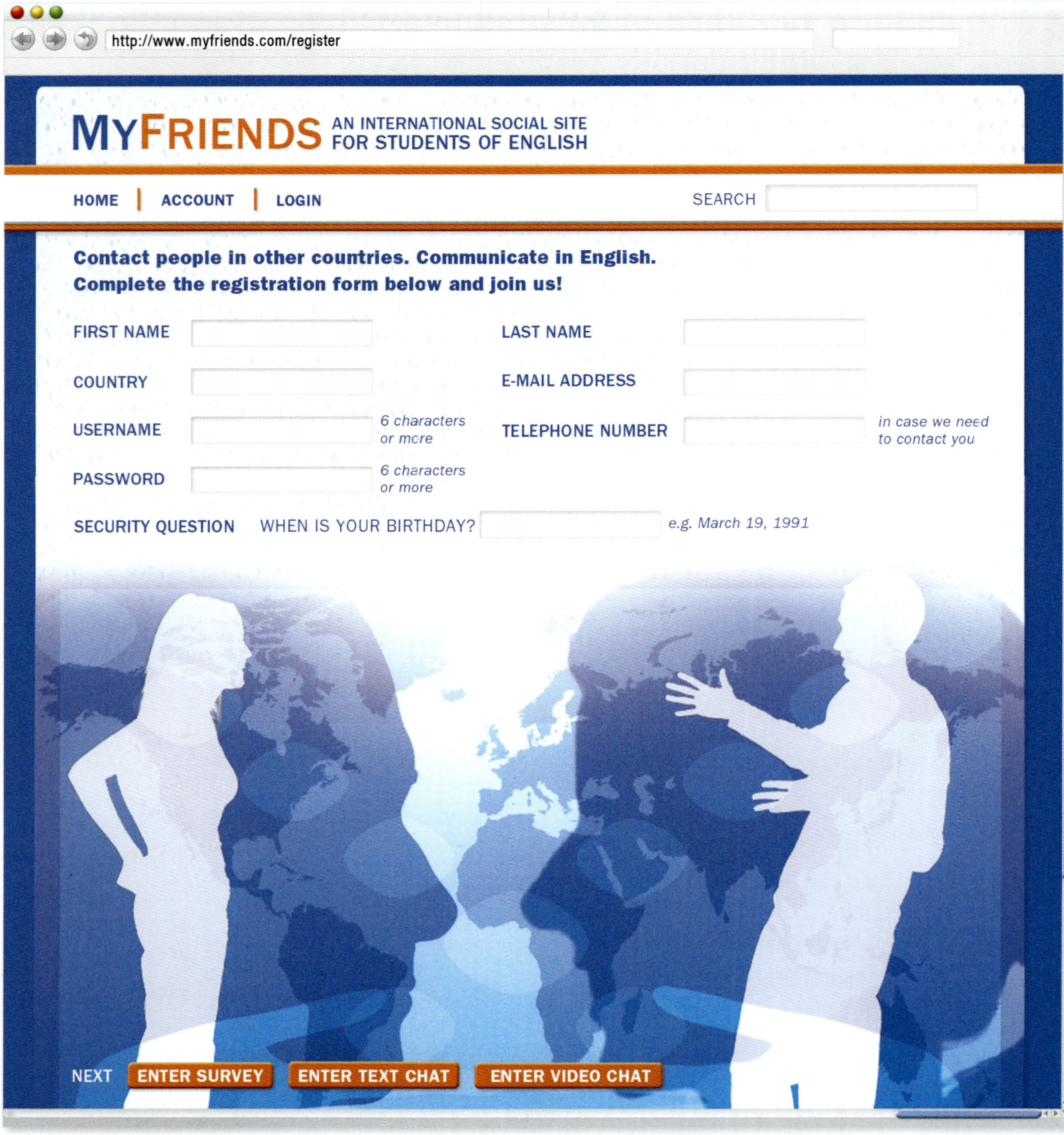

http://www.myfriends.com/register

MYFRIENDS AN INTERNATIONAL SOCIAL SITE FOR STUDENTS OF ENGLISH

HOME | ACCOUNT | LOGIN SEARCH

Contact people in other countries. Communicate in English.
Complete the registration form below and join us!

FIRST NAME ______ LAST NAME ______

COUNTRY ______ E-MAIL ADDRESS ______

USERNAME ______ *6 characters or more* TELEPHONE NUMBER ______ *in case we need to contact you*

PASSWORD ______ *6 characters or more*

SECURITY QUESTION WHEN IS YOUR BIRTHDAY? ______ *e.g. March 19, 1991*

NEXT ENTER SURVEY ENTER TEXT CHAT ENTER VIDEO CHAT

B Complete the online registration with your personal details. Invent a username and password.

2 **Reading:** recognizing cognates

Many words are similar in different languages. Look for these words when you read.
Use them to help you understand the text.

A Read the survey on the next page. Circle the words you recognize. How many words are similar in your language?

B Complete the survey.

http://www.myfriends.com/survey

MYFRIENDS AN INTERNATIONAL SOCIAL SITE FOR STUDENTS OF ENGLISH

HOME | ACCOUNT | LOGIN SEARCH

MyFriends Personal Profile Survey

Find friends similar to you. We have students from all over the world.
Complete the survey with information about yourself and click send.

I'm an English student in … a school. ◯ a university. ◯ a language institute. ◯

Reason for studying English:

academic studies ◯ work ◯ fun ◯

Academic or professional areas:

mathematics ◯	languages ◯	economics ◯	history ◯	science ◯
literature ◯	management ◯	art ◯	engineering ◯	finance ◯
education ◯	medicine ◯	business ◯	geography ◯	other ◯

Special interests:

music ◯	art ◯	dance ◯	literature ◯	travel ◯
sports ◯	animals ◯	ecology ◯	history ◯	politics ◯

SEND

Vocabulary: useful questions

3

A Listen and repeat the questions.

- Can you help me?
- Can you speak more slowly?
- How do you say that in English?
- Can you spell that?
- Can you repeat that?
- What does that mean?

B For each picture, say which questions are possible. Check with a partner.

1

2

3

4 Grammar: *be*—statements and *yes/no* questions

A Language in context Read this online chat. Complete the statements.

To: Paige <paige_smith@chat.com>

Masahiko: Hi! I'm Masahiko. I'm from Japan, and I'm 20 years old. And you?

Paige: My name's Paige. I'm 21, and I'm from New York. Are you from Tokyo?

Masahiko: No, I'm not, I'm from Kyoto.

Paige: Is Kyoto a big city?

Masahiko: Yes, it is! It's very big.

EMOTICONS BLOCK

1 Masahiko is from ____________.

2 Paige is ____________ years old.

B Notice Read the chat in Exercise A again. Complete these tables.

Statements				
Affirmative			**Negative**	
I	(1) _____ *(I'm)*	*from New York.*	*I am not (I'm not)*	*from Tokyo.*
You	*are (You're)*		*You are not (You aren't)*	
He/She/It	(2) _____ *(He's/She's/It's)*		*He/She/It is not (He isn't)*	
We	*are (We're)*		*We are not (We aren't)*	
They	*are (They're)*		*They are not (They aren't)*	

Yes/No questions		Short answers
(3) _____ *you*	*from Kyoto?*	*Yes, I am. / No, I'm not.*
Is he/she/it		*Yes, he/she/it is. / No, he/she/it isn't.*
Are we		*Yes, we/they are. / No, we/they aren't.*
Are we/they		

Watch out!
✔ Yes, we are.
✘ Yes, we're.

Watch out!
✔ I am 20 years old.
✘ I have 20 years.

C Practice Circle the correct options.

1 Jack and Madison *are* / *am* in Europe.

2 *Is* / *Are* you a music student?

3 John *isn't* / *aren't* here.

4 We *are* / *is* university students.

5 *Is* / *Am* she 19 years old?

6 Ed and Isabelle *isn't* / *aren't* from the U.S.

7 I *are* / *am* 22.

8 *Is* / *Are* Eva from Spain?

D **Now you do it** Work in pairs. Choose two of the people below. Role-play a conversation like the one in Exercise A.

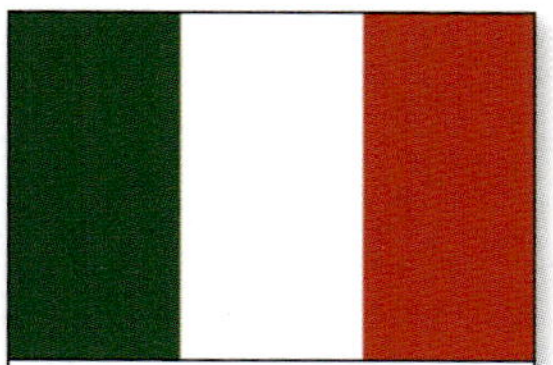

Sebastian, 19
Rome, Italy
university student

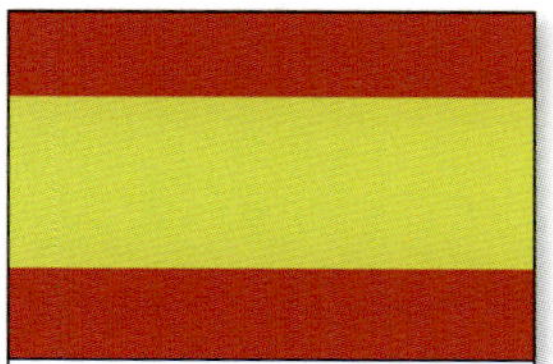

Ana, 24
Madrid, Spain
teacher

Devesh, 23
Delhi, India
office worker

Isabela, 27
São Paulo, Brazil
doctor

Pronunciation: the alphabet

5

A Listen to the alphabet. Notice that some letters have similar sounds. Write each letter in the correct category.

~~A~~ ~~B~~ ~~C~~ D E ~~F~~ G ~~H~~ ~~I~~ J K ~~L~~ M N ~~O~~ P ~~Q~~ ~~R~~ S T U V W X Y Z

/eɪ/	/i/	/e/	/aɪ/	/ju/	/oʊ/	/ɑr/
A, H	*B, C*	*F, L*	*I*	*Q*	*O*	*R*

B Work in pairs. Choose a word from this unit, or another English word you know. Spell it for your partner to guess the word.

Speaking: using polite language

6

Use *excuse me, thank you, thanks, you're welcome,* and *please* to be polite in English.

A Listen to the conversation below. Underline the polite language.

Laura: Excuse me. Can I get your information, please? What's your name?
Paula: It's Paula Lebowski.
Laura: Can you spell your last name, please?
Paula: It's L-E-B-O-W-S-K-I.
Laura: Thanks. Now, what's your e-mail address?
Paula: It's paulal@mail.com.
Laura: And your phone number?
Paula: It's (339) 414-2870.
Laura: Thank you very much.
Paula: You're welcome.

B Make a mini class directory in your notebook. Work in groups. Ask your classmates for their information. Include their first name, last name, e-mail address, and phone number. Use polite language.

How to say it

In e-mail addresses:
@ say *at*
. say *dot*

7 **Vocabulary:** ordinal numbers

A Write the correct number next to each word.

first 1st	seventh ______	eleventh ______
fourteenth ______	sixth ______	fifteenth ______
fourth ______	nineteenth ______	third ______
tenth ______	thirtieth ______	twenty-fifth ______
twelfth ______	second ______	fifth ______
thirteenth ______	ninth ______	
twentieth ______	eighth ______	

B Complete these sentences.

1 The last day of December is the ______________________ .

2 Today is the ______________________ .

3 Next Friday is the ______________________ .

4 The last day of February is the ______________________ .

5 The last day of April is the ______________________ .

6 My birthday is on ______________________ .

How to say it

We say:

Tuesday is the second.

Tuesday is October second.

We write:

Tuesday is October 2.

8 **Grammar:** *be*—information questions

A Language in context Listen to the conversation below. Circle true (*T*) or false (*F*).

Philip: Excuse me, can you answer some questions for my school project?

Lisa: Sure.

Philip: First of all, what's your name?

Lisa: Lisa Jackson.

Philip: And where are you from?

Lisa: Denver, Colorado.

Philip: How old are you, Lisa?

Lisa: I'm 20.

Philip: And when is your birthday?

Lisa: August 14.

Philip: Thank you. Now, I have a few more questions. What is your favorite …?

1 Lisa is from a town called Jackson.	T	F
2 She is 20 years old.	T	F
3 Her birthday is in August.	T	F

B Notice Read the conversation in Exercise A again. Complete this table.

Question word	Use	Example
(1) _what_	things	(5) ______ your name?
(2) ______	places	(6) ______ you from?
(3) ______	dates	(7) ______ your birthday?
(4) ______	someone's age	(8) ______ you?

C Practice Read these answers. Write questions.

1 A: _How old are you_ ? B: I'm 21. And you?
2 A: ______ ? B: I'm from Argentina. What about you?
3 A: ______ ? B: My last name is Alvarez.
4 A: ______ ? B: September 8.
5 A: ______ ? B: My brother? He's 30 years old.
6 A: ______ ? B: His name is George.

D Now you do it Ask your classmates questions to complete this table.

Find someone ...	Name
with a birthday in the same month as yours.	
from another town or country.	
with a last name beginning with the same letter as yours.	

Language use: listening to a voicemail message 9

A Listen to this voicemail message. Circle the correct options.

1 The message is from ...
a) Laura. b) Paula. c) Carla.
2 Her birthday is on August ...
a) 8. b) 18. c) 28.
3 Her party is at the ... Club.
a) Clinton b) Klinton c) Clintern
4 Her party is at ... o'clock.
a) five b) nine c) seven

B Work in pairs. Follow the instructions below.

- Student A, it's your birthday! Think about the date, place, and time of your party. Call your friend and leave a message.
- Student B, listen to the message and write the details.
- When you finish, switch roles.

Unit 1

lifeSkills

Information and research: understanding forms

- Identify the type of form.
- Complete the parts you understand.
- Ask for help with parts you don't understand.

A Where do you complete forms in English? Match the phrases to the correct picture.

a) at a hotel **b)** at the airport **c)** on a Web site **d)** at a language institute

1 ☐

2 ☐

3 ☐

4 ☐

B Read these forms. Circle the correct type of form. Then listen and complete the missing information.

Adelphi Palace
1404 Park View
San Diego California 93209-8568

Tel: (858) 349-8629
Fax: (858) 202-9998
E-mail: parkview@californianet.com

Full Name *Adolfo Mahuad* Date of Birth *5/12/1985*

Date of Arrival *June 17* Date of Departure ______

Smoking room ☐ Non-smoking room ☑

Single room ☑ Double room ☐

1 This is *a hotel registration form / a library application form.*

http://www.payment.com/

MAKE A PAYMENT

CARDHOLDER Adolfo Mahuad E-MAIL ADDRESS adolfom1991@mymail.com

CARD NUMBER 497233433321717 CARD TYPE VISA

SECURITY CODE ______ EXPIRATION DATE 12/31/2020

2 This is *a library registration form / a credit card payment form.*

C Look at this immigration form for the U.S. Complete the information in items 1–5.

U.S. Department of Justice
Immigration and Naturalization Service

OMB 1115-0077

Admission Number

Welcome to the United States

220390931 09

I-94 Arrival/Departure Record - Instructions

This form must be completed by all persons except U.S. Citizens, returning resident aliens, aliens with immigrant visas, and Canadian Citizens visiting or in transit.

Type or print legibly with pen in ALL CAPITAL LETTERS. Use English. Do not write on the back of this form.

This form is in two parts. Please complete both the Arrival Record (Items 1 through 13) and the Departure Record (Items 14 through 17).

When all items are completed, present this form to the U.S. Immigration and Naturalization Service Inspector.

Item 7 - If you are entering the United States by land, enter **LAND** in this space. If you are entering the United States by ship, enter **SEA** in this space.

Form I-94 (04-15-86)Y

Admission Number

220390931 09

Immigration and Naturalization Service

I-94
Arrival Record

1. Family Name
2. First (Given) Name
3. Birth Date (Day/Mo/Yr)
4. Country of Citizenship
5. Sex (Male or Female)
6. Passport Number
7. Airline and Flight Number
8. Country Where You Live
9. City Where You Boarded
10. City Where Visa Was Issued
11. Date Issued (Day/Mo/Yr)
12. Address While in the United States (Number and Street)
13. City and State

Departure Number

220390931 09

Immigration and Naturalization Service

I-94
Departure Record

14. Family Name
15. First (Given) Name
16. Birth Date (Day/Mo/Yr)
17. Country of Citizenship

See Other Side

STAPLE HERE

D Work in pairs. Role-play asking each other questions about the other information on the form.

How to say it

Excuse me. Can you help me, please?

What does ... mean?

What do I put here?

Can you please tell me what ... means?

I'm sorry, I don't know.

Reflect...

Forms are important, so always ask for help if you don't understand. What are some ways to ask for help?

Language Wrap-up

1 Vocabulary

A Complete these conversations with words from the box. (5 points)

slowly	repeat	say	help	spell

1 A: Can you ________________ me? This is very difficult. B: Yes, of course.

2 A: How do you ________________ that in English? B: You say, "Excuse me."

3 A: Can you speak more ________________, please? B: Yes, I'm sorry.

4 A: How do you ________________ your name? B: It's P - E - N - E - L - O - P - E.

5 A: Sorry, can you ________________ that, please? B: Yes. P - E - N - E - L - O - P - E.

B Write each of the ordinal numbers in parentheses as a word. Check your spelling! (5 points)

1 Today is August ________________. *(2nd)*

2 Tomorrow is the ________________. *(3rd)*

3 The ________________ of July is American Independence Day. *(4th)*

4 November ________________ is an important day in the U.K. *(5th)*

5 The ________________ is the last day of August. *(31st)*

8–10 correct: I can ask useful questions and use ordinal numbers.
0–7 correct: Look again at Sections 3 and 7 on pages 9 and 12. **SCORE: /10**

2 Grammar

Sandra is from the U.S. She is introducing herself to a new friend in Argentina. Read her e-mail. Circle the correct options. (10 points)

To: carolina_smith@mymail.com
From: sandra_brown@mymail.com
Subject: Hi

Hi Carolina,

My name (1) *am / is / are* Sandra and I (2) *am / is / are* from Chicago, in the U.S. I'm 19—my birthday (3) *am / is / are* in May. I (4) *am / is / are* a student in college—I study biology. My friends at school (5) *am / is / are* Tina, Sophie, and Lisa. Tina and Sophie (6) *am / is / are* 19 and Lisa is 18. What about you? (7) *What / Where / How* old are you? (8) *What / Where / When* is your birthday? (9) *What / Where / When* exactly are you from in Argentina—is it Buenos Aires? (10) *What / Where / When* are the names of your friends?

I hope you answer my e-mail!

Your new friend,

Sandra

8–10 correct: I can use *be* in statements and ask questions to get information about people.
0–7 correct: Look again at Sections 4 and 8 on pages 10 and 12. **SCORE: /10**

What do You Do?

A Match these famous people to their main occupation.

1 

2 

3 

A movie director

B singer

C actor

B Each person also does another activity. Who is ...

1 a clothing designer?
2 a musician?
3 a pilot?

1 **Vocabulary:** occupations

A Match the occupations to the pictures.

1 ___G___ taxi driver
2 ______ teacher
3 ______ actor
4 ______ firefighter
5 ______ police officer
6 ______ soldier
7 ______ doctor
8 ______ engineer
9 ______ lawyer
10 ______ writer

A

B

C

D

E

F

G

H

I

J

B Which of these occupations are dangerous? Number the red boxes from 1 (very dangerous) to 10 (not dangerous).

C Work in pairs. Compare your choices. Do you agree or disagree?

A: *My number one is …*
B: *I agree.*

D Work in pairs. Number the occupations again from 1 (very interesting) to 10 (not interesting). Number the blue boxes.

Pronunciation: two-syllable nouns

2

A Listen to the words. Notice that the first syllable in each word is stressed.

doctor teacher lawyer

B Work in pairs. Practice saying these words. Make sure you stress the correct syllable. Listen and check.

student teacher writer actor soldier doctor lawyer

Grammar: articles *an* and *a*

3

A Language in context Read this text. What job or jobs does each person do?

B Notice Look at the text in Exercise A again. Circle the correct options.

1 We use *a* before *singular nouns* / *plural nouns*.

2 We use *an* before singular nouns that begin with *a vowel* / *a consonant*.

3 Before plural nouns, we *use* / *don't use a* or *an*.

C Practice Write *a* or *an* where necessary.

1 James is ______ soldier.

2 Wayne and Darren are ______ teachers.

3 I want to be ______ artist.

4 Are you ______ police officer?

5 Lauren and I are ______ musicians.

6 Are you ______ singer?

7 Michelle is ______ taxi driver.

8 Harry isn't a doctor—he's ______ engineer.

Watch out!

✔ My mother is a teacher.

✘ My mother is teacher.

D Now you do it Work in pairs. Ask and answer questions about the people in the pictures in Exercise A.

A: *What does he do?*

B: *He's a …*

4 Vocabulary: family members

A Look at this picture. Say what Rita, Greg, Brenda, Bob, and Joshua do.

1 ________ 2 ________ 3 *mom* 5 ________ 6 ________ 7 ________

4 *parents*

B Listen and write the correct word from the box under each family member.

grandpa	brother	boyfriend	dad	~~parents~~	~~mom~~	grandma

C Listen and match.

1 parents	a) sister
2 brother	b) girlfriend
3 mom and dad	c) granddaughter
4 boyfriend	d) children
5 grandparents	e) husband
6 wife	f) daughter

Watch out!

✔ My parents are Tom and Jessica.

✘ My fathers are Tom and Jessica.

5 Listening: listening for specific information

Read the task before you listen. Think about what information you need. For example, is it a name or a place? Listen carefully for this information.

A Read these statements about Simon. Circle the correct type of missing information.

1 Simon is a ________________ .

The missing information is *his last name* / *his occupation*.

2 His ________________ is a chef.

The missing information is *a family member* / *a place*.

3 He says his job is ________________ .

The missing information is *an adjective* / *a noun*.

4 He starts his job at ________________ o'clock.

The missing information is *a name* / *a time*.

B Listen and complete the sentences in Exercise A with one word.

C Listen to this conversation between Simon and a friend. Answer the questions.

1 What is the woman's name? ______________________

2 What does she do? ______________________

3 What does her brother do? ______________________

4 What time is it? ______________________

Language use: reading a celebrity biography

6

A Many actors come from acting families. Is this true in your country?

B Read this biography. Answer the questions.

SPANISH STAR IN HOLLYWOOD

by Emma Spires

Javier Bardem is an actor from Spain. He comes from an acting family. Some of his relatives are actors. His mother (Pilar Bardem) is an actor, and his uncle (Juan Antonio Bardem) was a movie director. His brother Carlos and his sister Monica are both actors.

Javier is famous in both the Spanish-speaking world and the English-speaking world. He has many awards, including an Oscar and a Golden Globe award for his role in *No Country for Old Men.*

1 Where is Javier Bardem from? ______________________

2 What do his brother and sister do? ______________________

3 What awards does Javier Bardem have? ______________________

C Work in groups. Do you know people who have similar occupations to other members of their family? Think of as many as you can and compare.

My sister, my dad, and my mom are engineers.

Watch out!

✔ engineer

✘ engineer

Watch out!

✔ I have four relatives in the U.S.

✘ I have four parents in the U.S.

Unit 2

7 Grammar: possessive nouns—'s and s'

A Language in context Match the pictures to the phrases.

1 ☐

2 ☐

3 ☐

a) the Smiths' house **b)** the sisters' bicycle **c)** Brittany's cell phone

B Notice Look at the pictures and phrases in Exercise A again. Complete this table.

Singular nouns	Plural nouns
Add (1) ______ e.g., *Brittany* = *Brittany's*	Add (2) ______ e.g., *sisters* = *sisters'*

Richard's a car mechanic.
= *Richard is ...*

Richard's car is here.
= belonging to Richard

Watch out!

✔ Jack and Sally are students.

✘ Jack and Sally are student's.

C Practice Use the prompts to write sentences.

1 our children / jobs / very interesting ______ *Our children's jobs are very interesting.*

2 Richard / brother / mechanic ______

3 my parents / new car / blue ______

4 Mr. Johnson / sister / here? ______

5 Michael / parents / doctors? ______

6 Victoria / mom / lawyer ______

7 Amy / sister / not / doctor ______

8 the Coen brothers / new movie / great ______

D Now you do it Say what these people's relatives do. Work in pairs.

Sofia's dad is a movie director.

Ralph and Joseph Fiennes

Owen and Luke Wilson

Eleanor, Sofia, and Francis Ford Coppola

Language use: talking about family

8

A Listen to the conversation below. Answer the questions.

Sam: Tell me about your family.
Lauren: Well, my brother James is a mechanic.
Sam: And your sister?
Lauren: Nicole's a teacher.
Sam: Are they married?
Lauren: Yes, my brother's wife is a taxi driver, and Nicole's husband is a police officer.
Sam: What about your parents?
Lauren: Mom's an assistant in a store, and Dad's a lawyer. What about your family?

1 What does Lauren's sister do?
2 What does her mom do?

B Draw your family tree in your notebook.

C Work in pairs. Ask and answer questions about each other's relatives and their occupations.

A: *What does your mom do?*
B: *She's a …*

Watch out!
✓ Lauren's sister
✗ the sister of Lauren

Writing: understanding the mechanics

9

Use a capital letter at the beginning of every sentence, and a period, exclamation point, or question mark at the end of every sentence. Also use capital letters for the word *I*, for the names of people and places, for countries, nationalities, and languages, and for months and days of the week.

A Find the mistakes in each sentence and underline them.

1 My brother is in egypt.
2 Today is february 14.
3 My sister and i are dentists
4 I start my new job on wednesday.
5 How do you say this in english
6 How old is your brother, peter?

B Write sentences to answer these questions. Be careful with capital letters and punctuation.

1 What do you do? ______________________
2 What day is it today? ______________________
3 What month is it? ______________________
4 Who is your favorite relative? ______________________

lifeSkills

Thinking and problem-solving: categorizing

- Understand the purpose for categorizing.
- Categorize the items using relevant characteristics.
- Use the information to make a decision.

A **Look at the Web site on the next page. Who is it for?**

This Web site is for people who … **a)** want to find their ideal job. **b)** want to find someone to do a job.

B **Work in pairs. Write these careers in different categories. Each career can be in more than one category.**

architect

computer engineer

sales manager

designer

journalist

mechanic

creative jobs: ______________________

well-paid jobs: ______________________

office jobs: ______________________

jobs working with others: ______________________

jobs outside an office: ______________________

jobs working from home: ______________________

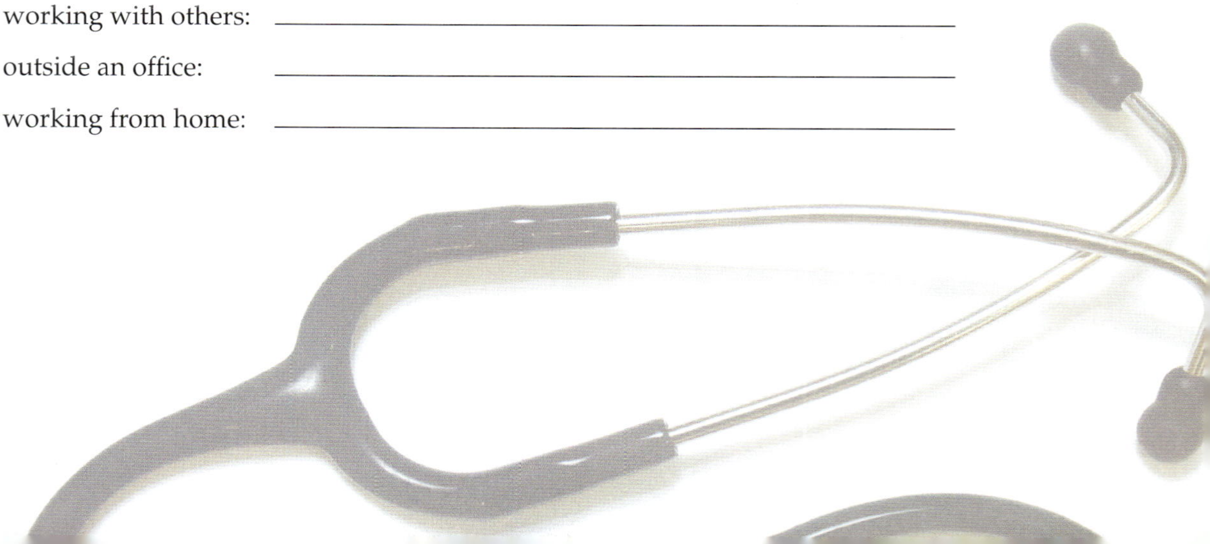

C Complete this questionnaire for yourself. You can choose more than one answer.

http://www.dreamcareers.com/

DREAMCareers

HOME | HELP | CONTACT US | SEARCH

DREAM CAREERS questionnaire

THE PERFECT WAY TO FIND YOUR IDEAL CAREER

Name: ____________ **Age:** ______

1 Where is your ideal place to work? at home ◯ in an office ◯ outside an office ◯

2 What is the best time for you to work? in the morning ◯ in the afternoon ◯ at night ◯

3 What is a good way for you to work? with one or two other people ◯ alone ◯ in a large group ◯

4 What is important to you? helping people ◯ a good salary ◯ job security ◯ interesting work ◯

5 What words describe you? careful ◯ independent ◯ hard-working ◯ creative ◯ patient ◯

D Work in pairs. Compare your answers and complete the sentence below for your partner. Use the jobs in Exercise B to help you.

My partner's perfect for the job of

______________________ .

E Tell your classmates about your job recommendation for your partner.

Sally is perfect for the job of…

Reflect…

Putting things into categories helps you think about the similarities and the differences between them.

Unit 2

Language Wrap-up

p128–129

1 Vocabulary

Look at Mark's family tree. Then complete these sentences with one word. There are five jobs and five family words. (10 points)

1 Edward and Eileen are Mark's ____________ .

2 His dad, Edward, is an ____________ .

3 His mom, Eileen, is a ____________ .

4 Mary and Jessica are Mark's ____________ .

5 Ian is his ____________ .

6 Mary is a ____________ .

7 Jessica is a police ____________ .

8 Sarah is Mary's ____________ .
She's four years old .

9 George and Betty are Mark's ____________ .

10 George is a taxi ____________ .

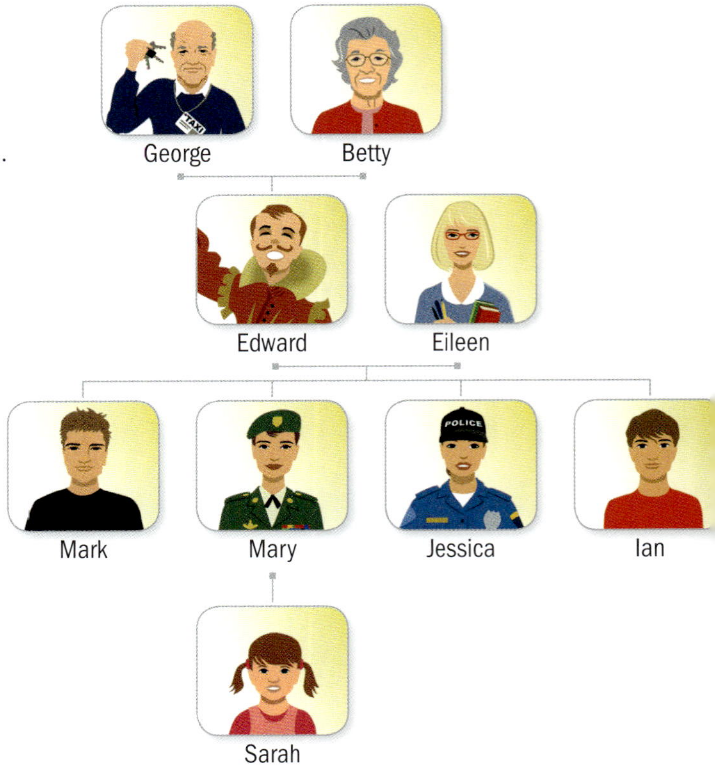

8–10 correct: I can talk about occupations and family members.
0–7 correct: Look again at Sections 1 and 4 on pages 18 and 20. **SCORE: /10**

2 Grammar

A Read these facts about famous people and their families. Complete the sentences with *a* or *an* where necessary. (5 points)

Julio Iglesias is (1) ______ famous singer. His sons, Enrique and Julio Iglesias Jr. are (2) ______ singers, too. Michael Douglas's wife, Catherine Zeta Jones, is (3) ______ actor. Michael's father, Kirk Douglas, is also (4) ______ actor. He is very famous, too. The Baldwin brothers, Alec, Daniel, William, and Stephen are all (5) ______ actors!

B Read these facts about famous people. Add five apostrophes. (5 points)

1 Madonnas full name is Madonna Louise Ciccone.

2 George Clooneys father is a famous TV host and writer.

3 Paul McCartneys daughter is Stella McCartney. She is a famous fashion designer.

4 Alec Baldwins brothers are all actors. His brothers names are Stephen, William, and Daniel.

8–10 correct: I can use articles and possessive nouns to talk about occupations and families.
0–7 correct: Look again at Sections 3 and 7 on pages 19 and 22. **SCORE: /10**

Down Time

Unit 3

A For each day, check (✓) the times when you are free.

B Read the information below and answer the question.

The average free time in the U.S. each week for teenagers (15–19 years old) is 37.8 hours. The average for young adults (20–24 years old) is 35.2 hours.

How much free time do you have in total each week?

________ hours

1 Grammar: simple present—statements and *yes/no* questions

A **Language in context** Listen to the conversation below. What does May buy?

Jake: Wow! You have a lot of music on your computer.
May: Yeah. I buy MP3s online. My brother likes music, too, but he doesn't buy MP3s. He buys CDs. He has hundreds.
Jake: Do you like this song?
May: Yes, I do.
Jake: Me, too. Let's play it!

B **Notice** Read the conversation in Exercise A again. Complete this table.

Affirmative	Negative	Yes/No questions	Short answers
I *You* *We* *They* *buy CDs.*	*I* *You* *We* *They* *don't buy CDs.*	(3) ______ *I* *you* *we* *they* *buy CDs?*	*Yes,* *I* *you* *we* *they* (4) ______ .
He *She* (1) ______ *CDs.* *It sounds great.*	*He* *She* (2) ______ *buy CDs.* *It doesn't sound great.*	*Does* *he* *she* *buy CDs?* *Does it sound great?*	*No,* *Yes,* *he* *she* *it* *doesn't.* *does.*

With verbs ending in a consonant + *y*, the form after *he/she/it* ends in *–ies*:

e.g., *I/You/We/They stu**dy** ...*
*He/She/It stud**ies** ...*

The verb *have* is irregular:

e.g., *I/You/We/They **have** a lot of CDs.*
*He/She/It **has** a lot of CDs.*

C **Practice** Complete these sentences using the verbs in parentheses in the correct form.

1 Chelsea ________________ (*like*) jazz music.
2 My brother and I ________________ (*collect*) stamps.
3 ________________ you ________________ (*have*) MP3s on your computer?
4 Anna ____________________________ (*not have*) a lot of CDs.
5 ________________ Sara and Kathy ________________ (*listen*) to hip-hop?
6 The store ________________ (*have*) a big collection of classical music.
7 ________________ Richard ________________ (*play*) the guitar?
8 My sister ____________________________ (*not buy*) a lot of music.

Watch out!
✔ He likes music.
✘ He like music.

D **Now you do it** Work in pairs. Ask and answer questions about these things.

- hip-hop
- stamps
- cars
- the piano

A: *Do you listen to hip-hop?*
B: *Yes, I do. Do you?*
A: *No, I don't.*

How to say it
Do you listen to ...?
Do you like ...?
Do you play ...?
How about you?

Watch out!
✔ Do you like music?
Yes, I do.
✘ Do you like music?
Yes, I like.

Pronunciation: third person *–s* 2

A Listen to the verbs. Notice that the third person -s endings are pronounced differently.

1 /z/	listens	does	plays
2 /s/	wants	likes	
3 /ɪz/	watches	practices	relaxes

B Work in pairs. Practice saying these sentences. Listen and check.

1 My dad listens to the radio every morning.
2 Jason practices the piano after school.
3 Mom likes walking the dog.
4 Our class sometimes watches English movies.

Reading: recognizing cognates p8 3

In English, long words that look difficult are often cognates in other languages. Look at long words carefully. You can often figure out what the word means even if you recognize only part of it.

A Read this text. Find all the words which are similar to words in your language. Compare the words you find with a partner.

HERE'S SOME ADVICE!

Do you want a celebrity hobby?

Celebrities have free time – and they have money! So what hobbies do they have, and can you do the same thing?

British singer **Rod Stewart** builds model railroads!
• Use your imagination to create your own railroad systems! You can even get model passengers for your trains!

Sarah Michelle Gellar (Buffy in *Buffy the Vampire Slayer*) loves antique books.
• First editions are valuable and they cost a lot. Go to book fairs or look in second-hand stores for books in good condition.

Brad Pitt is interested in architecture, and he's helping with reconstruction in New Orleans.
• You probably can't build real houses, but you can design your own living space. Decorate your house or room with art and objects that you like.

B Match each celebrity to the correct picture.

A

B
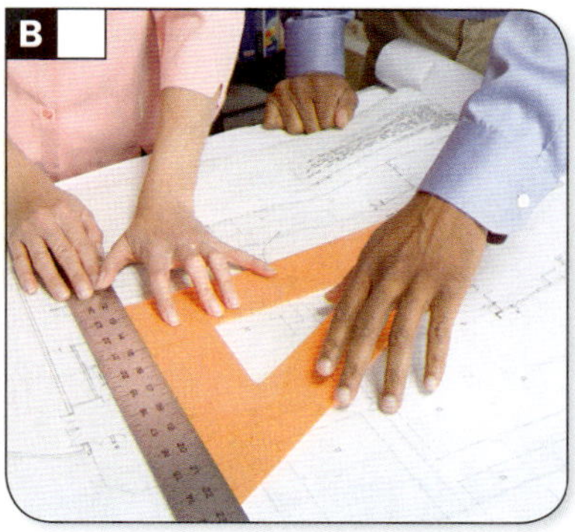

C

1 Rod Stewart   2 Sarah Michelle Gellar   3 Brad Pitt

4 **Language use:** listening to a radio show

A Look at this picture. What do you think the radio show is about?

B Listen to this discussion. Circle the correct person for each question.

1 *Angelica / Victor* likes sports games.

2 *Angelica / Victor* doesn't like puzzle games.

3 *Angelica / Victor* plays driving games.

4 *Angelica / Victor* likes the story in *Automania*.

C Work in groups. Discuss these questions.

Do you play video games?

YES →
What video games do you play?
What's your favorite game? Why?
What video games don't you like?

NO →
What other games do you play?
Do you watch or play sports?
What's your favorite sport? Why?

5 **Vocabulary:** free time activities

A Check (✓) the free time activities you do once a week or more. How much time do you spend on each one in a typical week?

listen to music ☐
_______ hours

watch TV ☐
_______ hours

go online ☐
_______ hours

play sports ☐
_______ hours

see friends ☐
_______ hours

go bowling ☐
_______ hours

work out ☐
_______ hours

play video games ☐
_______ hours

go to the movies ☐
_______ hours

B Work in pairs. Compare your free time activities. Who prefers doing things with other people? Who prefers doing things alone?

I listen to music about five hours a week.

Grammar: simple present—information questions

6

A Language in context Read this ad. What is the TV show about?

WE WANT TO MAKE A TV SHOW ABOUT REAL FANS!

Are you a TV fan?

What shows do you watch every day?

When do you watch them?

Why do you like them?

Where do you watch TV?

Who do you like to watch on TV?

Tell us and you can be the next TV star!

B Notice Read the ad in Exercise A again. Complete this table.

Question word	Auxiliary	Subject	Verb
What/Where When/Why/Who	___________	*I/you/we/they*	*watch do go ...?*
	does	*he/she/it*	

Watch out!

✔ Where do you go in your free time?

✘ Where you go in your free time?

C Practice Use the prompts to write questions.

1 why / you like basketball?

____

2 when / Tom go to the gym?

____

3 where / they meet for coffee?

____

4 what / you want to do this evening?

____

5 who / go out with in your free time?

____

6 what / Jane do in her free time?

____

How to say it

What do you do in your free time?

Who do you play/go/watch ... with?

Why do you like it?

Because it's fun/interesting/exciting.

D Now you do it Work in pairs. Ask and answer questions about your free time activities. Are they similar or different?

7 Speaking: asking for opinions

When you want to know what somebody thinks, you can use different phrases to ask for their opinion.

A Listen to this conversation. What are they discussing?

B Listen again. Check (✓) the phrases you hear asking for opinions.

- ☐ And you?
- ☐ What's your opinion?
- ☐ Do you agree?
- ☐ What do you think?
- ☐ How about you?

C Work in groups. Talk about your opinions of these kinds of movies. Use phrases from Exercise B to ask about each other's opinions.

A: *I like comedies. How about you?*
B: *No, I prefer action movies.*
A: *Why?*
B: *Because comedies are silly. Action movies are exciting.*

science-fiction movies

comedies

action movies

love stories

8 Vocabulary: personality adjectives

A Check (✓) *A* or *B* to complete this quiz. Calculate your score. Then compare with a partner.

Are you an introvert or an extrovert?

TAKE OUR QUIZ AND FIND OUT!

	A		B	
1	I love parties.	☐	I like quiet evenings at home.	☐
2	It's great to meet new people.	☐	I get nervous with people I don't know.	☐
3	I hate being alone.	☐	I like being alone.	☐
4	I tell lots of jokes.	☐	I don't know many jokes.	☐
5	I have lots of friends.	☐	I have a few close friends.	☐
	Number of As: ________		Number of Bs: ________	

B Read about your personality type. Do you think it is correct? Compare with a partner.

more "A"s	more "B"s
You are an extrovert. You are **confident** and **sociable.** You love parties. You are **popular** and have lots of friends. You are **funny** and you like telling jokes.	You are an introvert. You are **shy**, and you don't like big parties very much. You have a few close friends, and you are very **loyal.** You are **considerate** and think about other people.

C Work in pairs. Think of someone you know well. Describe them to your partner. Use the adjectives from Exercise B in **bold**.

My sister is an extrovert. She's very sociable. She likes ...

Language use: writing about yourself and your interests

9

A How well do you know your classmates? Choose one person and say three things you know about them.

B Read this web page. What does this Web site do?

http://www.meetup.com/home

meetUP

register · home · help · login

Welcome to **meetUP**. The idea is simple. We find new friends for you where you live. Tell us about yourself and your interests. What do you like doing in your free time? Music, sports, movies—we have thousands of people with the same interests.

NEW MEMBERS

Hi, I'm Ben. I'm 24 years old. I study in the evenings, but I'm free on weekends. I'm very sociable and I love parties! I like sports—tennis is my favorite! I don't like computers or video games. I prefer being with friends!

CLICK TO CONTACT BEN

Hello. I'm Yara. I'm 21 and I live with my parents. I don't have a lot of free time because I study a lot! I like going to the movies with my friends. I also like listening to music. I'm a little shy, but I'm a loyal friend!

CLICK TO CONTACT YARA

C Write about yourself for the Web site. Describe your personality and your interests.

Watch out!

✔ I like listening to music.

✘ I like listen to music.

D Put your descriptions on the wall. Read your classmates' descriptions. Find two people with interests similar to yours.

Self-direction and learning:
understanding your learning style

- Identify your main learning style.
- Use it to help you learn new things.
- Try other styles to support your learning.

A **Choose a new skill you want to learn. Circle how you want to learn it.**

☐ play a musical instrument

☐ draw or paint

☐ juggle

☐ speak a new language

I want to learn my new skill …

a) in a class. **b)** with a friend. **c)** alone.

B **Complete this learning style questionnaire. Calculate your scores.**

LEARNING STYLE QUESTIONNAIRE

1 Which skill did you choose in Exercise A?

- ■ (red) play a musical instrument
- ■ (green) draw or paint
- ■ (blue) juggle
- ■ (yellow) speak a new language

2 Think about learning English. How do you prefer to learn new words?

- ■ (red) I say words.
- ■ (green) I draw pictures.
- ■ (blue) I act out words.
- ■ (yellow) I write words.

3 How do you like to learn English grammar?

- ■ (red) by listening to my teacher
- ■ (green) by looking at diagrams
- ■ (blue) by imagining myself in a situation
- ■ (yellow) by reading grammar rules

4 What do you like doing in your English classes?

- ■ (red) listening
- ■ (green) reading
- ■ (blue) speaking
- ■ (yellow) writing

5 Which school subject do you prefer?

- ■ (red) music
- ■ (green) art
- ■ (blue) drama
- ■ (yellow) literature

Total number of …

- ■ (red) ____________
- ■ (green) ____________
- ■ (blue) ____________
- ■ (yellow) ____________

C **Work in pairs. Follow these instructions to learn the words using your preferred learning style.**

- Student A, look at the first group of words. Student B, look at the second group.
- Check the definitions of the words and phrases in a dictionary or ask your teacher.
- Read the instructions below that match your main color from Exercise B.
- Follow the instructions to learn the words. You have five minutes.

Student A	Student B
• satellite dish	• fracas
• current affairs	• domain name
• broadcast	• crate

Musical

Say the words and the definitions aloud.

Listen carefully to how the words sound.

Try to remember each word and sound together.

Visual

Imagine each word in your mind.

Draw a picture to represent each word.

Try to remember each word and picture together.

Kinesthetic

Imagine a situation where you need to use each word.

Do an action connected to that situation.

Try to remember each word and action together.

Linguistic

Write each word and think of the definition.

Repeat each word a few times.

Try to remember each word and definition together.

D **Work in pairs. Cover the words in Exercise C and test each other. How many words do you remember?**

How to say it

Tell me one of the words.

The first word is ...

What's the next word?

What does it mean?

E **Look at your scores in Exercise B. What is your second color? Use the instructions above to learn the new words below. After a few minutes, test each other. Which of the two ways of learning do you prefer?**

- puzzle • pastime • laid-back • couch potato

Reflect...

You can always improve your different learning styles. Which one do you want to improve in the future?

Language Wrap-up

1 Vocabulary

A **Complete these sentences with phrases from the box. (5 points)**

watch TV	play sports	go online	listen to music	see friends

1 I have a computer in my bedroom and I ______________ to buy music.

2 I ______________ every day. I love rap and hip-hop.

3 I ______________ in my free time. I like soccer and hockey, but I prefer basketball.

4 I ______________ after school. We go bowling, go to the movies, or meet for coffee.

5 I ______________ in the evening. I like *The Simpsons* and *American Idol*.

B **Read about Anna and Katy. They are sisters, but they are very different. Match the adjectives to the explanations. (5 points)**

1 Anna is very shy.
2 Katy is very funny.
3 Anna is very considerate.
4 Katy is very sociable.
5 Anna is very loyal.

a) She makes everyone laugh with her jokes.
b) She thinks about other people.
c) Her friends can trust her. She never says a bad thing about them.
d) She loves parties and being with a lot of friends.
e) She doesn't like meeting new people.

8–10 correct: I can talk about free time activities and about people's personalities.
0–7 correct: Look again at Sections 5 and 8 on pages 30 and 32. **SCORE:** /10

2 Grammar

Mark and Jody are at Beth's party. Write the verbs in parentheses in the correct form of the simple present. (10 points)

Mark: Hi, I'm Mark.

Jody: Oh, hi. I'm Jody. So, how (1) ______________ you ______________ (*know*) Beth?

Mark: She (2) ______________ (*play*) volleyball with my sister.

Jody: Oh, cool. What (3) ______________ you ______________ (*do*), Mark?

Mark: I go to the university. I (4) ______________ (*study*) French and German. And what about you?

Jody: I (5) ______________ (*work*) with my dad. He (6) ______________ (*have*) a restaurant.

Mark: Oh, yeah? (7) ______________ you ______________ (*like*) it?

Jody: It's OK, but I (8) ______________ (*not want*) to do it my whole life. My mom (9) ______________ (*not think*) it's a good job.

Mark: Oh, really? What (10) ______________ she ______________ (*want*) you to do?

Jody: She wants me to be a doctor.

8–10 correct: I can use the simple present to talk about myself and to ask questions about other people.
0–7 correct: Look again at Sections 1 and 6 on pages 28 and 31. **SCORE:** /10

Day In, Day Out

Unit 4

A Read these sayings about time. Do you have similar sayings in your first language?

Time waits for no man.

Time flies when you are having fun.

Don't put off until tomorrow what you can do today.

The early bird gets the worm.

B Work in pairs. Do you agree with the sayings in Exercise A?

Life's too short to worry.

1 **Vocabulary:** telling time

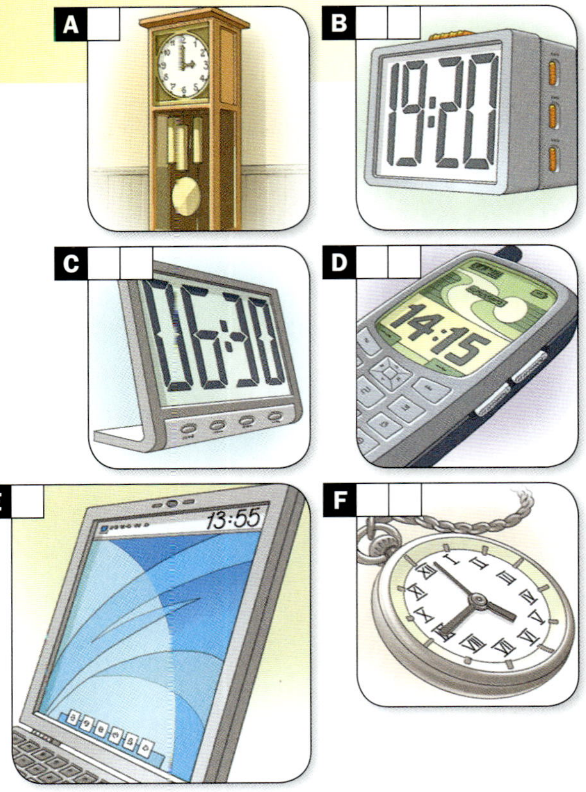

A **Match these sentences to the correct times. Some times match to more than one sentence.**

1 It's twenty after seven.
2 It's five to two.
3 It's three (o'clock).
4 It's a quarter after two.
5 It's six-thirty.
6 It's a quarter to six.
7 It's seven-twenty.
8 It's half past six.
9 It's two-fifteen.
10 It's five forty-five.

B **Listen and check your answers to Exercise A.**

C **Work in pairs. Say what time you usually do these things on weekdays.**

- get up
- leave for school/work
- get to school/work
- have lunch
- have dinner
- go to bed

A: *What time do you have lunch?*
B: *I have lunch at (about) two. And you?*

2 **Language use:** reading a magazine article

A **Read this article. What is the difference between larks and owls?**

What Type of Bird Are You?

One in ten people is a lark. About two in ten are owls and enjoy staying up very late. If you like to get up early, have coffee and read the paper, you're probably a lark. Owls often don't eat breakfast and have to hurry to get to work in the morning. If you do laundry or surf the Internet at midnight, you're probably an owl.

Larks and owls often have different jobs. Emergency room doctors, for example, work more at night. They are usually owls. Writers and artists are often larks. For example, cartoonist Scott Adams is a lark. "I never try to do any creating past noon," he says. "And I only exercise in the late afternoon. I draw from 6 a.m. to 7 a.m. Then I write for a few hours."

Larks	Owls
best before noon	best after 6 p.m.
go to bed early	stay up late
favorite meal: breakfast	favorite meal: dinner
drink coffee in the morning	drink coffee in the evening

B **Work in pairs. Ask and answer these questions.**

1 Are you a lark or an owl? Why?
2 What time of day do you like to work or study?
3 What time of day do you like to relax?

Grammar: frequency adverbs

A Language in context Listen to the conversation below. Answer the questions.

Rick: I'm always so busy! I **never** have any free time. I'm **always** at work in the morning and I **usually** study in the afternoon. What about you?

Alicia: I don't work, so I **often** get up late. I **sometimes** study in the morning and I relax in the afternoon. I almost always go out in the evening.

Rick: I **rarely** have time to go out—maybe just once a month. But I love to go to the movies.

Alicia: Me, too! Do you want to go to the movies this weekend?

Rick: Sure. That sounds great.

1 Who does a lot every day? ____________

2 Who doesn't do a lot every day? ____________

B Notice Read the conversation in Exercise A again. Complete this diagram with two of the words in **bold**. Then answer the questions.

0% ⟵⟶ 100%

never ____________ sometimes often usually ____________

1 Do these words come before or after the verb *be*? ____________

2 Do these words come before or after other verbs? ____________

Watch out!
✔ I am always happy.
✘ I always am happy.

C Practice Write sentences about how often Rick does each of these activities. Use each frequency adverb from Exercise B once.

be late for class	0 times a week	(1) *He is never late for class.*
cook at home	6 times a week	(2) ____________
chat online	4 times a month	(3) ____________
drive to work	every work day	(4) ____________
play video games	1 time a year	(5) ____________
watch the news	4 times a week	(6) ____________

D Now you do it Work in groups. Ask and answer questions to find out how often people in your group do each activity in Exercise C. Then report back to the whole class.

A: *In our group, Victor and Lisa rarely cook at home.*
B: *Vera always cooks at home.*

How to say it
How often do you ...?
How often are you ...?

4 **Pronunciation:** days of the week

A Listen and repeat. Notice that the stress is always on the first syllable.

Monday   Tuesday   Wednesday   Thursday   Friday   Saturday   Sunday

B Work in pairs. Practice saying these sentences. Make sure you stress the correct syllable. Listen and check.

1 I work from Monday to Friday.
2 I go to the gym on Tuesdays and Wednesdays.
3 My favorite day of the week is Saturday.
4 I think Sundays are boring.

5 **Listening:** listening for specific information p20

A Look at the pictures and listen to the interviews. Match each picture to the day the woman does the activity.

A

B

C

D

E
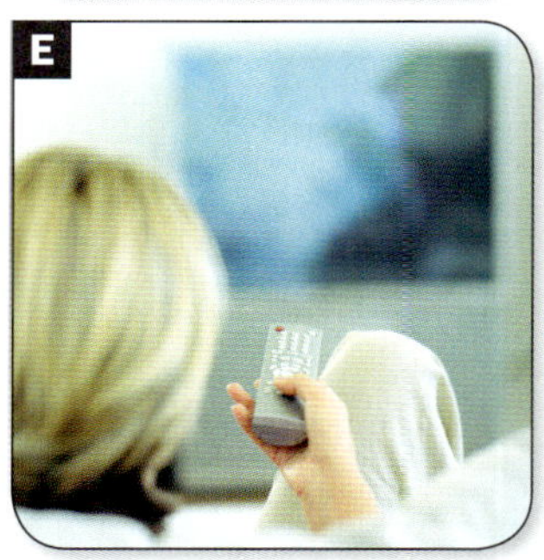

F

_____ Monday
_____ Tuesday
_____ Wednesday
_____ Thursday
_____ Friday
_____ Saturday

B Listen to the rest of the interview. What does the woman do on Sundays? Check (✓) the activities she mentions.

- [ ] have breakfast
- [ ] go for a walk
- [ ] do the housework
- [ ] read the newspaper
- [ ] meet friends
- [ ] go to the gym
- [ ] watch TV
- [ ] have lunch
- [ ] cook

C Work in pairs. Describe your usual weekend routine. Do you and your partner do similar or different things on weekends?

On Saturdays, I usually get up late. I …

Vocabulary: prepositions of time

6

A Read what this woman says about her routine. Circle the correct options to complete each explanation.

"I usually work until five o'clock. I get home at six. On weekdays, I go to bed early. I usually watch TV until bedtime. On Fridays, I always go out after work. I see friends in the evenings. Sometimes, I don't get home before 3 a.m.! I sleep late on Saturday mornings."

1 We use *until* / *before* / *after* to say when we stop doing something.

2 We use *until* / *before* / *after* to say at a later time.

3 We use *until* / *before* / *after* to say at an earlier time.

B Read the text in Exercise A again. Write two more examples of your own for each category in the table below.

on	at	in	before	after	until
Fridays	*five*	*the evening*	*3 a.m.*	*work*	*bedtime*

C Complete these sentences with one word.

1 My English class starts ___________ two-thirty.

2 Let's go out ___________ Thursday.

3 I always brush my teeth ___________ I take a shower.

4 I study ___________ about 10 p.m., and then I go to bed.

5 See you ___________ the morning!

6 My dad usually plays soccer ___________ work.

Language use: talking about interesting activities

7

A Listen to the conversation below. Answer the questions.

Janet: You look unhappy, Mark.

Mark: Well, I'm just a little bored with my routine. Every week is the same.

Janet: Hmm. Well, I try to do something interesting every week.

Mark: Like what?

Janet: Well, on Tuesdays I go to acting classes. And on Fridays, I do karate.

Mark: Oh, that sounds fun!

Janet: Come to karate with me this week.

Mark: OK, thanks!

1 Why is Mark unhappy? ___________________________

2 What interesting things does Janet do? ___________________________

B Walk around the class and ask each person to tell you two interesting or unusual things they do each week. Find out as much as you can.

A: Do you do anything unusual each week?

B: On Tuesdays, I take a dance class.

C Tell the rest of the class about any interesting or unusual things your classmates do.

Grammar: clauses with *until*, *before*, *after*

A Language in context Read what this man says. Why does he do these things?

"I'm pretty superstitious. I stay in the dressing room until I'm the last one. Then I follow the others. I always touch the grass before I start to play. It brings me luck. After I do all of that, I always play well!"

B Notice Read the examples from Exercise A in the table. Circle the correct options to complete the explanations.

To talk about the order of events ...		
after	*After I do all of that, I always play well.*	We use *after* with the (1) *first* / *second* event.
before	*I always touch the grass before I start to play.*	We use *before* with the (2) *first* / *second* event.
To talk about the duration of events ...		
until	*I stay in the dressing room until I'm the last one.*	We use *until* to talk about an event that continues to another event or a specific time.

I always play well after I do all of that.

After I do all of that, I always play well.

C Practice Complete these sentences with *before*, *after*, or *until*.

1 Dan has his piano lesson at seven. He has dinner at nine.

Dan has his piano lesson ___________ he has dinner.

Dan has dinner ___________ he has his piano lesson.

2 I get home. Then I call my friends.

I call my friends ___________ I get home.

3 Christy studies every day. She stops when she finishes all her school work.

Christy studies every day ___________ she finishes all her school work.

4 I go to the office. Then I have coffee.

I have coffee ___________ I go to the office.

I go to the office ___________ I have coffee.

Watch out!

✔ I get dressed before I have breakfast.

✘ I get dressed before have breakfast.

D Now you do it Work in pairs. Ask and answer questions about what you do before and after you do these things.

- leave the house in the morning
- do your homework
- go out in the evening with friends
- go to bed

A: *What do you do before you leave the house in the morning?*
B: *Before I leave the house in the morning, I ...*

Writing: understanding the mechanics p23

A sentence expresses a whole idea. Sentences in English always have a subject and a verb. When there is no other subject, we use *it*.

A Check (✓) the correct sentences. Rewrite the incorrect sentences.

1 ☐ Friday my favorite day. ______________________

2 ☐ It is twenty to seven. ______________________

3 ☐ Is cold today. ______________________

4 ☐ I an unusual routine. ______________________

5 ☐ My dad gets up at 4 a.m. ______________________

6 ☐ Is an interesting job. ______________________

B Read about an unusual routine. Find three sentences that are incorrect and underline them. Explain why they are incorrect and suggest changes.

Amy Robinson is a radio DJ. She presents the breakfast show. She has an unusual routine. Gets up at about four-thirty and drives to the studio. She has breakfast at the studio and she does the show from six until nine. Is a tiring job! After the show, she goes home and she sleeps for an hour. In the afternoon, prepares the next show. She goes to bed at eight o'clock. She does that six days a week!

C Think of someone (a member of your family, a celebrity, etc.) with an unusual routine. Write a few sentences in your notebook describing what you think he/she does on a typical day.

D Work in pairs. Read each other's sentences. Do the two people have similar or different routines?

E Read your partner's sentences again. Is every sentence correct? Help your partner find any mistakes.

Organization and planning: managing your time

- Understand any problems you have with managing your time.
- Write a to-do list and categorize each task.
- Decide on the best order for the tasks.

A How well do you manage your time? Complete this quiz. Compare your answers in pairs.

It's time to think about time!

Some of us are born to be late and others are always on time. Take our fun quiz to find out which you are!

1 How do you feel about time?

a) I never have enough time!
b) Sometimes I don't have time to do everything, but usually it's OK.
c) Time? I have lots of it!

2 Do you arrive on time for things?

a) Yes, always.
b) Sometimes, but not always.
c) No, I'm always late!

3 Do you often have nothing to do?

a) No, I'm always busy.
b) Sometimes.
c) Yes, I do.

4 How often do you check the time?

a) I'm too busy to look at the clock!
b) Never. I don't have a watch.
c) Often. I like to know what time it is.

5 You have something important to do. How do you feel?

a) I'm not worried because there's lots of time.
b) Help! I have a thousand things to do today!
c) Forget it. I can do it tomorrow.

6 How do you work or study?

a) I just work until I finish.
b) I waste time on other things.
c) It's difficult! I never have time to finish my work or study.

Now add up your score:

1.	a **3**	b **2**	c **3**
2.	a **1**	b **2**	c **3**
3.	a **3**	b **2**	c **1**
4.	a **3**	b **1**	c **2**
5.	a **2**	b **3**	c **1**
6.	a **2**	b **1**	c **3**

My total

6–10
You have a lot of time —because you don't do important things! Manage your time better and you can achieve more.

11–15
You have a good attitude about time. With a little time management, you can do even more.

16–18
You need to manage your time and give yourself time to relax!

B Make a list of everything you want or need to do in the coming week. Estimate the time you need for each one. Look at the example below.

C Work in pairs. Ask and answer questions about your lists. Read this key and write a letter next to each task.

A: This is absolutely necessary.

B: This is important, but not absolutely necessary.

C: This isn't very important, but I want to do it.

D: This isn't important at all.

How to say it

Is this important?

How important is this?

It's very important!

I don't really need to ... Let's write D.

D Write your things to do in order. For each day of the week, write A things first, followed by B things, etc. Think about the time you have and consider moving some things from one day to another.

Sunday	Monday	Tuesday	Wednesday	Thursday	Friday	Saturday

E Work in pairs. Compare your daily to-do lists. Can you do everything in the time you have?

Reflect...

How does categorizing tasks help you to organize your time?

Language Wrap-up

p130–131

1 Vocabulary

A **Rita is talking about her day. Look at the time on each watch. Then complete these sentences with a verb and the correct time. (6 points)**

1 I ______________ to school at a ______________.

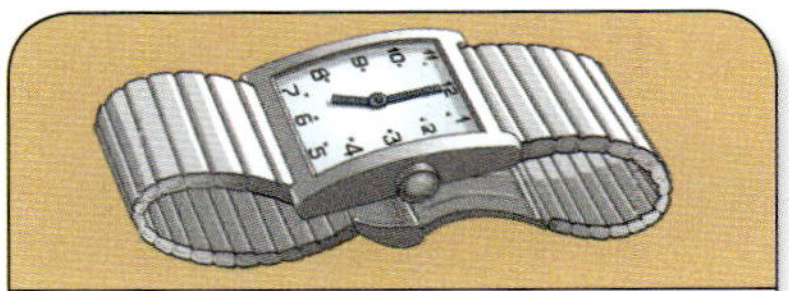

2 I ______________ dinner at ______________.

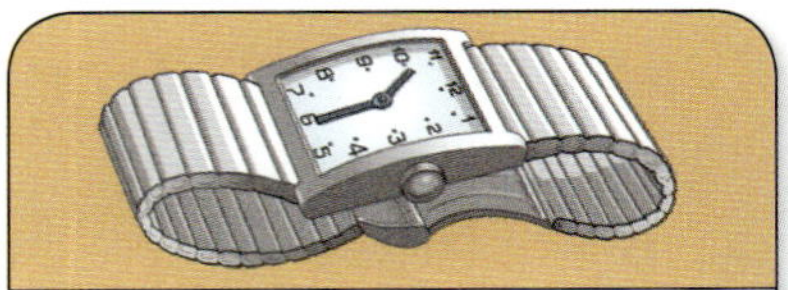

3 I ______________ to bed at ______________.

B **Rita is talking about other parts of her day. Circle the correct prepositions. (4 points)**

1 I always have breakfast *at* / *before* / *after* / *until* I go to school.

2 I sometimes go for coffee with friends *until* / *at* / *after* / *on* school.

3 *On* / *In* / *Until* / *At* Saturday nights, I use my computer or watch a movie *before* / *after* / *on* / *until* midnight and then I go to bed.

8–10 correct: I can tell the time and use prepositions to talk about what I do in a typical day.
0–7 correct: Look again at Sections 1 and 6 on pages 38 and 41. **SCORE: /10**

2 Grammar

A **Read this text about how frequently five people play video games. Write their names in the correct order on the scale. (5 points)**

When Leo comes home from school, he always plays video games. His sister, Marina, sometimes plays with him, but she prefers going online to talk to friends. David often plays video games after school, but not every day. His sister, Lola, never plays. She thinks video games are boring. Samuel rarely plays video games, but he likes one soccer game that he plays with his brother.

100% ←――――――――――→ 0%

1 __________ 2 __________ 3 __________ 4 __________ 5 __________

B **Rewrite the sentences with *before, after,* or *until*. Use the correct punctuation. (5 points)**

1 Leo has dinner and then he plays games on his computer.

____ *(before)*

2 Marina talks to friends online. She stops when it's time for bed.

____ *(until)*

3 David does his homework. Then he plays video games.

____ *(after)*

4 Lola watches TV. She stops when she goes to bed.

____ *(until)*

5 Samuel plays a video game and then he listens to music.

____ *(after)*

8–10 correct: I can use frequency adverbs and time clauses to talk about when and how often people do things.
0–7 correct: Look again at Sections 3 and 8 on pages 39 and 42. **SCORE: /10**

Here, There, and Everywhere!

A Match the places to the events.

a) Colombia
b) China
c) France
d) the U.S.

1 Dragon Boat Festival

2 marathon

3 film festival

4 book fair

B Which events look fun to you? Why?

1 **Language use:** listening to a news report

A Listen to the start of a news report. Circle the correct options.

1 Buñol is near the city of ...
a) Valencia. **b)** Murcia.

2 La Tomatina festival happens in ...
a) September. **b)** August.

B Listen to the rest of the report. Circle the correct options.

1 Mary speaks to a man from …
a) Spain. **b)** Britain. **c)** Germany.

2 All the people go to … to have breakfast.
a) the main square **b)** the park **c)** their houses

3 At eleven o'clock, everyone …
a) goes home. **b)** throws tomatoes. **c)** eats tomatoes.

4 The festival continues for …
a) two weeks. **b)** two days. **c)** two hours.

C Give your opinion. What do you think about the Tomatina festival? Do you like festivals in general?

How to say it

It sounds interesting/fun.

I love/hate festivals.

2 **Grammar:** *there is/there are* with *some*, *any*, *several*, *a lot*, *many*

A Language in context Read about the Caribana festival. Answer the questions.

www.travelquestions.com

Helen asks "Are there any interesting festivals in Canada this year? Is there one in eastern Canada? I live in New York."

Jan answers "There is a cool festival in Toronto every year. It's called Caribana and it's all about Caribbean culture. There are a lot of visitors to the city. They all come to dance, eat, and have fun! The carnival parade starts in the afternoon in the main square. There's a big picnic in the park and there are several calypso music competitions. There are also some other competitions, including a food competition. There aren't many tickets for the festival left. It's a good idea to buy them soon!"

1 Where is the Caribana festival? 2 When does the parade start?

B Notice Read the examples from Exercise A in the table. Circle the correct options in the sentences on the next page.

Affirmative	*There is a cool festival in Toronto every year.*
	There are several calypso music competitions.
	There are also some other competitions.
Negative	*There aren't many tickets for the festival left.*
Questions	*Are there any interesting festivals in Canada this year?*
	Is there one in eastern Canada?

1 We use *there is / there are* to talk about one thing.
2 We use *there is / there are* to talk about more than one thing.
3 We use *some / any* with *Are there …?* and *There aren't.*
4 We use *some / any* with *There are.*
5 We use *several* and *many* to talk about *one thing / more than one thing.*

Watch out!
✔ There are a lot of people.
✘ There is a lot of people.

C Practice **Circle the correct options.**

1 There *isn't / aren't* any festivals in my country in November.
2 *Is / Are* there any food festivals in your town?
3 In Mazatlan, there *is / are* a carnival in February.
4 There are *several / any* carnivals around the world every year.
5 Are there *any / a* dance competitions during the festival?
6 There *is / are* a lot of people in the parade.

D Now you do it **Work in pairs. Choose a festival in your city or country. Describe it for your partner to guess. Then switch roles.**

A: *It's in August. There are musicians. There's a parade.*
B: *The music festival!*

Vocabulary: places and attractions in a city 3

A **Listen to this automated message about the Chinese New Year festival. Circle the places on the map that the speaker mentions.**

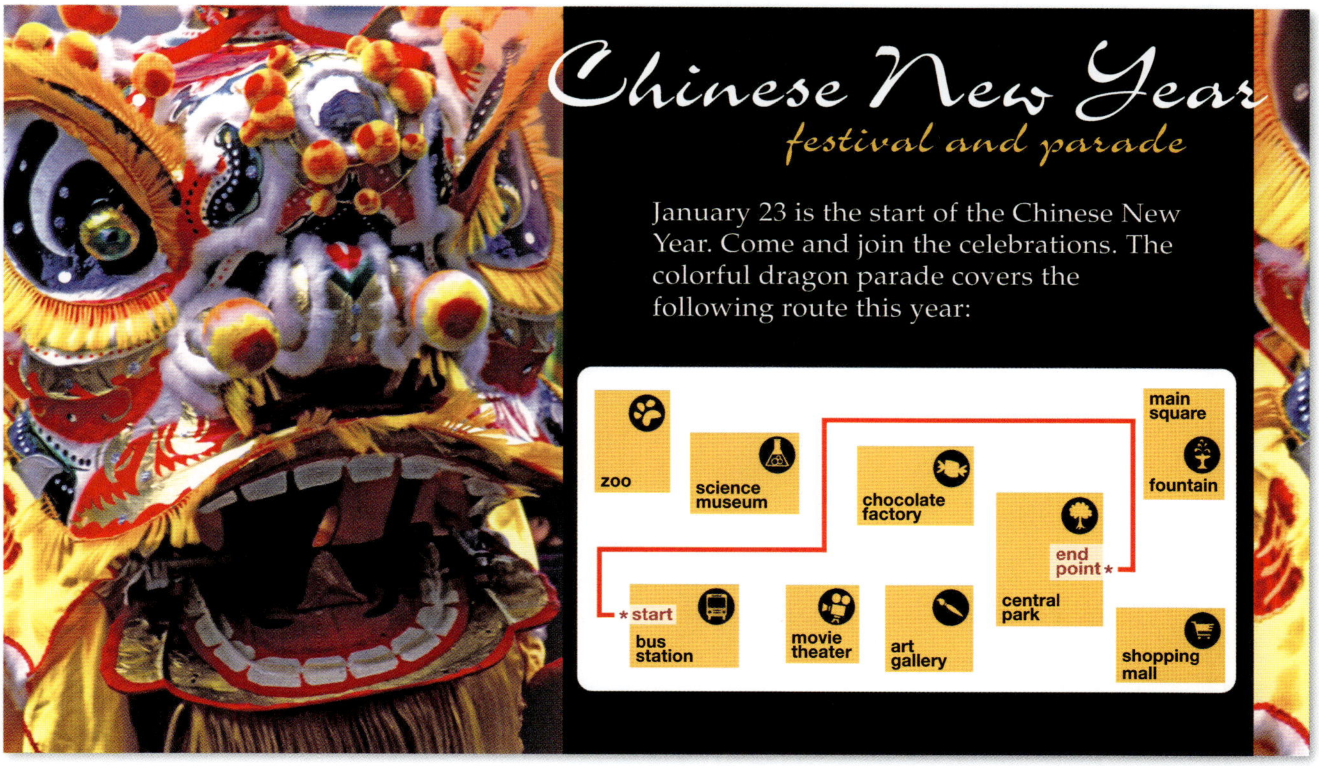

B **Work in pairs. Answer the questions.**

1 How many places on the map are also in your town?

A: *There's a zoo.*
B: *Yes, and there are several …*

2 How many other places in your town can you name in English?

A: *There are a lot of banks.*
B: *And there's a history museum.*

4 **Pronunciation:** compound nouns

A **Listen and repeat. Notice that in compound nouns (noun + noun), the first word is stressed.**

museum—science museum   mall—shopping mall   factory—chocolate factory   theater—movie theater

B **Work in pairs. Make new compound nouns for places in your city. Then practice saying the words.**

1 history museum   2 train station   3 car factory

________ museum   ________ station   ________ factory

5 **Reading:** reading for the main idea

When you read a text, think about these questions. What is the general topic? What is the writer saying about the topic?

A **Read these texts quickly. Circle the main topic.**

a) neighborhoods **b)** festivals **c)** families

Emile

"I live in a quiet area in Paris. I like living there because it's very friendly and there are several stores and cafés. The only problem is that it's a little boring sometimes because there aren't any clubs. There's a good stadium, though. I often go to sports events."

Melissa

"I live in Singapore, in a very busy neighborhood. I don't like it because it's noisy and there's lots of traffic. There's a shopping mall near my house, and I go there a lot. There are also museums and a movie theater in the area, but I don't have time to go to them. There's a good food festival in April, though."

Kostas

"I live in Oia on the island of Santorini. My neighborhood is pretty big. A lot of my neighbors are members of my family! There aren't many stores, but there's a small art gallery, a movie theater, and a gym. Oh, and there are a lot of great restaurants. I think it's a fantastic place to live."

B **Read the texts in Exercise A again. Decide whether each person has a positive or negative opinion of where they live.**

Emile: *positive / negative*

Melissa: *positive / negative*

Kostas: *positive / negative*

C **Work in pairs. Talk about your neighborhood. Do you like it? Why or why not?**

I like my neighborhood because it's small and …

Grammar: *should*

A Language in use Read this text. Circle where it is probably from.

What 3 things should you see in and around London?

We think you should definitely see ...

▶ Windsor Castle

The home of the Royal Family, just 40 minutes from London. You shouldn't visit on the weekends, though. It's very crowded.

▶ Harrods department store

You should definitely go to Harrods. Don't miss the food hall!

▶ Wembley Stadium

You should visit this famous stadium. Go on the tour. It's great.

The text is probably from ...

a) a newspaper. **b)** a guidebook. **c)** a magazine.

B Notice Read the examples from the text in the table. Circle true (*T*) or false (*F*).

Affirmative	*You should definitely go to Harrods.* *You should visit this famous stadium.*
Negative	*You shouldn't visit on the weekends.*
Questions	*What should you see in London?*

definitely = 100%
really = 80%
probably = 55%

Adverbs of certainty (*definitely*, *really*, and *probably*) usually come after the modal verb *should* and before *shouldn't* in statements:

e.g., *You should probably visit the museum.*

You probably shouldn't go to the zoo.

1 We use *do* in questions and negatives with *should*. T F

2 The contraction of *should not* is *shouldn't*. T F

C Practice Complete this conversation with *should* or *shouldn't*. Then listen and check.

Janet: Our trip to London is next week! I'm so excited! What (1) ____________ we do there?

Max: Well, I have a good guidebook here. It says we (2) ____________ see Windsor Castle, but we (3) ____________ visit the castle on the weekend. We (4) ____________ also visit Wembley Stadium. We (5) ____________ probably go on the tour of the stadium.

Janet: Good idea! We (6) ____________ definitely go to Harrods, too, and we really (7) ____________ miss the food hall. I can't wait!

D Now you do it Student A, you are a visitor to Student B's town or city. Ask Student B what places or attractions you should or shouldn't see. Give reasons. Then switch roles.

A: *What should I visit in your town?*

B: *I think you should definitely visit the art gallery. It's really interesting. You shouldn't visit the museum. It's small and very crowded.*

Vocabulary: locations and directions

A Read and match the sentences to the pictures.

1 Take the second street on the left.
2 Make a U-turn.
3 It's on Laurel Avenue.
4 It's next to the museum.
5 Follow the signs for the zoo.
6 It's across from the movie theater.
7 Turn left here.
8 Go over the bridge.
9 It's between the bank and the school.
10 Go straight ahead.
11 Take the first right.
12 It's on the corner of Mason Street and Laurel Avenue.

A 

B 

C 

D 

E 

F 

G 

H 

I 

J 

K 

L 

B **Look at this street map. Student A, you are at the main square. Student B, you are at the art gallery. Ask each other for directions to different places on the map.**

A: *How do I get to the zoo from here?*
B: *Go right on Main Street. Take the first street on the left. That's River Street. Then …*

How to say it

Excuse me, where is the …?
How do I get to …?
Is there a … near here?
Turn left/right on …

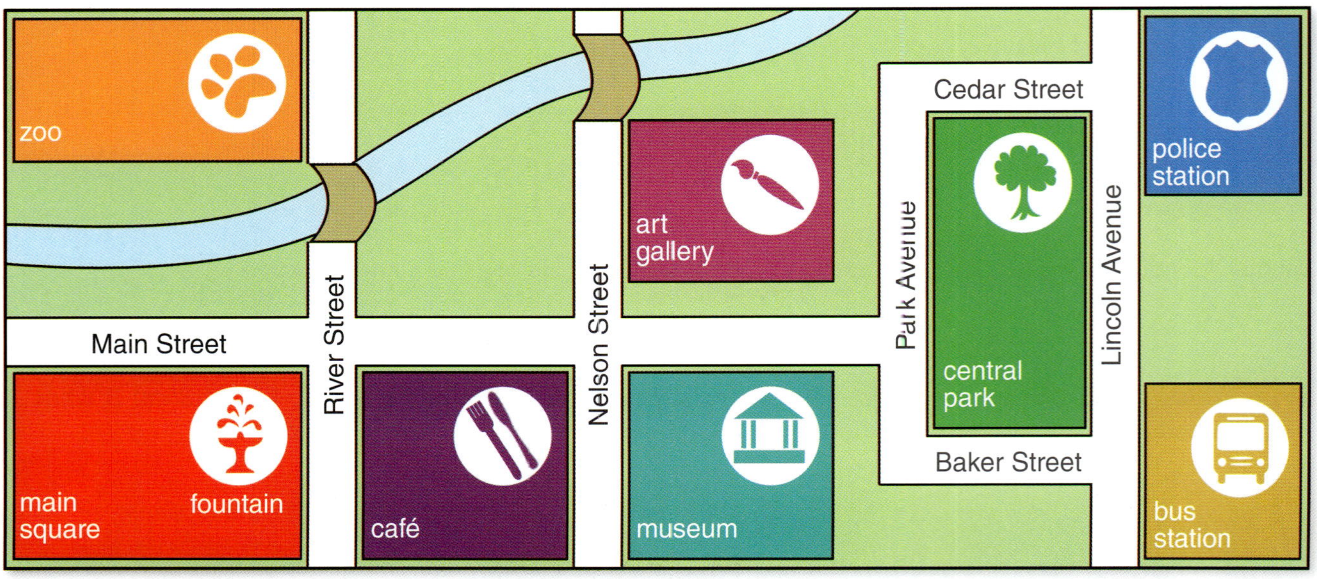

Speaking: repeating directions to check understanding

8

When you ask for directions, listen carefully and repeat the essential information to check that you understand.

A **Listen to the conversations below. Underline the information that Speaker A repeats.**

1

A: Excuse me, how do I get to the main square?
B: You take the first right, and go straight ahead. Then turn left on Post Street.
A: OK. First right, then left on Post Street.
B: That's right.
A: Thank you.
B: You're welcome.

2

A: Excuse me, is there a bank near here?
B: Yes, there's one on Fort Street.
A: Fort Street. OK. And how do I get there?
B: You go straight ahead, and take the third left.
A: Straight ahead, and take the second left.
B: No, not the second left, the third left.
A: Third left. OK, thanks.

B **Work in pairs. Take turns asking for directions to places in your town.**

A: *Excuse me, how do I get from ... to ...?*
B: *You take the ... It's on ...*

Language use: writing an e-mail

9

A **Read this e-mail from a friend. What does Avril need?**

To: my_friend@mymail.com
From: avril_wright@mymail.com
Subject: Directions

Hi!
Thanks for inviting me to the exhibition. I don't know where the art gallery is, exactly. I need directions from the bus station to the gallery. How do I get there?
Thanks a lot!
Avril

B **Look at the map in Section 7 again. Write an e-mail to Avril giving her directions in your notebook.**

How to say it

Hi, ...
OK. Here are the directions to ...
From ...
Then ...
Don't get lost!
See you soon.

lifeSkills

Thinking and problem-solving: establishing priorities

- Understand the criteria.
- List the options.
- Order the options according to the criteria.

A You see this comment about your city on a Web site. Read the comment and answer the questions.

http://www.i-travel.com/home

i-travel — The Web site for travel inspiration

Home | Login | Register | About *i-travel* | Search | Go

i-travel > travel forums > cities > **one day in ...**

Forum: one day in ...

Posted on: May 3 at 09:34 by Danny1992
Registered: 03/15/10
Posts: 5

Subject: Where to go? Help!
I'm in the city for one day next week and I don't know what to visit. I arrive at 7:00 in the morning and leave on the 8:00 p.m. bus. I don't have much money—only $40. Does anyone have any ideas?? Thanks!
Replies: 0
Reply <<previous next>>

1 How much time does Danny have in your city? ________________

2 How much money does Danny have to spend? ________________

B Work in pairs. In your notebook, make a list of the main attractions in your city. Write down as many as you can. Then write the cost and the time you need to visit each one.

What?	How much?	How long?

How to say it

I think you need ... hours.
I agree. There's also a ...
How long do you need to visit ...?
How much does the ... cost?
I think it costs $ ...
I think it's free.

C Think about organizing your options from Exercise B. Complete this *Top 5 Things to Do!* list for Danny with your partner. Decide why you think Danny should see or do these things. Remember that he only has $40 and 13 hours in your town/city.

Gregg's chocolate factory tour
Reason: It's cheap (only $12) and interesting

Top 5 Things To Do!

1.
   Reason:
2.
   Reason:
3.
   Reason:
4.
   Reason:
5.
   Reason:

D Write a short response to Danny.

http://www.i-travel.com/home

i-travel The Web site for travel inspiration

Home | Login | Register | About *i-travel* | Search | Go

Forum: one day in...

Posted on: May 4 at 14:21
Registered: 07/23/09
Posts: 12

Re: Where to go? Help!

Hello, Danny1992! There are lots of great things to do in my city.

You should definitely ______________________________
____

You should probably ______________________________
____

You should really ______________________________
____

Enjoy your stay!

Reply <<previous next>>

E Read your options to your classmates. Decide which ones make the best use of Danny's $40 budget and time.

Reflect...

In what other situations do you need to establish priorities?

Language Wrap-up

1 Vocabulary

A Look at this map. Complete the place names with words from the box. (4 points)

gallery
station
mall
theater

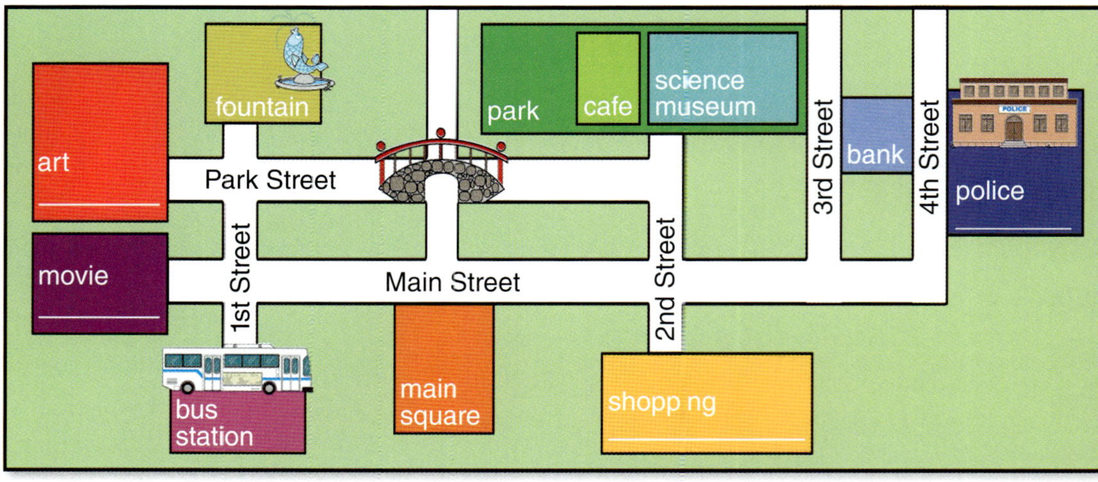

B Look at the map in Exercise A again and complete the sentences. (6 points)

1 You are at the bus station __________ 1st Street. Take the second right, go __________ the bridge, and turn left. Go straight ahead and the ______________ is in the park, __________ the café.

2 You are in the main square. Turn right and go straight ahead. Then take the third left. The ______________ is on the right ______________ the bank.

8–10 correct: I can talk about places and attractions in a city and ask for and give directions.
0–7 correct: Look again at Sections 3 and 7 on pages 49 and 52. **SCORE: /10**

2 Grammar

Read these contributions to a chat room. Circle the correct options. (10 points)

In Granada, there (1) *is / are* a fantastic Moorish monument—the Alhambra Palace. You (2) *should / shouldn't* visit in April or May. It's nice, but not too hot. The food in Spain is excellent and there (3) *is / are* a lot of restaurants. But you (4) *should / shouldn't* eat in restaurants near the Alhambra—they are very expensive.

Antigua is a beautiful city. There (5) *is / are* several pretty squares where you can have lunch or just drink coffee. If possible, you should (6) *find / go* a hotel in the main square. You (7) *should / shouldn't* travel in taxis in Antigua because it's small, and it's possible to walk everywhere.

Ko Samui is a fantastic island. There (8) *isn't / aren't* many cars and you can relax completely. The restaurants and cafés are very friendly and there (9) *is / isn't* a lot of good food. Sometimes there (10) *is / are* traditional dances.

8–10 correct: I can use *there is*, *there are*, and *should* to talk about places and to give advice.
0–7 correct: Look again at Sections 2 and 6 on pages 48 and 51. **SCORE: /10**

Different Strokes

Unit 6

A Check (✓) the things that are a big part of your life.

B Work in pairs. Compare the things that are a big part of your life. Do you have similar or different lifestyles?

A: *Eating is a big part of my life. I like going to restaurants, but I also like cooking at home.*

B: *Me, too. I don't usually go to restaurants, and I often cook at home.*

1 **Vocabulary:** lifestyle adjectives

A Look at these different lifestyles. Write each word from the box under the lifestyle it describes.

relaxing healthy boring stressful unhealthy wasteful green exciting

1 ______________

2 ______________

3 ______________

4 ______________

5 ______________

6 ______________

7 ______________

8 ______________

B Work in pairs. Say what type of lifestyle you and your family have. Say why.

A: *My mom has a healthy lifestyle. She plays sports and she eats healthy food.*

B: *Really? Well, my dad is 65 now, so his life isn't very ...*

2 **Language use:** reading personal profiles

A Read these profiles. Where do you think they come from?

a) an online dating agency **b)** a Web site about famous people **c)** an online English course

http://www.youandme.com/

You and me.com
Find your perfect date

home login register FAQs contact us search

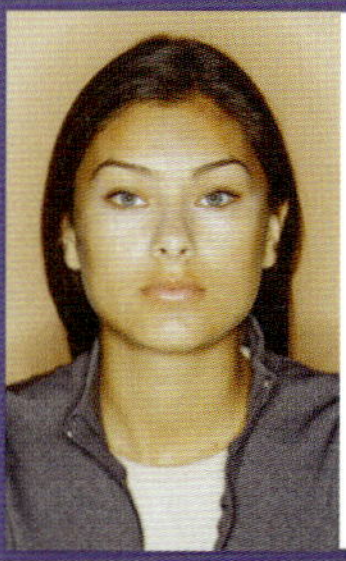

Name: Christina
Age: 19
Likes: reading; cooking; animals; going to the ballet
Dislikes: soccer; loud music; cold weather
My lifestyle is: healthy!
Right now: I am a university student.

Name: Guido
Age: 22
Likes: rock music; animals; fast food; surfing
Dislikes: studying; soccer; the winter
My lifestyle is: exciting!
Right now: I'm working in a music store.

B Work in pairs. Answer these questions.

1 What do Christina and Guido have in common?
2 In what ways are they different?
3 In your opinion, is it a good idea for them to date?

How to say it

She likes ... but he likes ...

They like ...

Grammar: present progressive

A Language in context **Listen to the conversation below. What does Jon hate?**

Jon: Hey, Daisy! What are you doing right now?
Daisy: Oh, hi, Jon! I'm studying for a math test.
Jon: Ugh! I hate math tests! What other subjects are you studying this semester?
Daisy: I'm taking an English class and a science class.
Jon: Me, too! Are you working this year?
Daisy: Yes, I am. I'm working in a café in town. It's fun.

B Notice **Read the conversation in Exercise A again. Complete this table. Then circle the best option to complete the rules.**

Affirmative	Negative	*Yes/ No* question	Short answer	*Wh-* question
I'm working.	*I'm not* (1) ______ .	*Am I working?*	*Yes, I* (3) ______ . *No, I'm not.*	*Where am I working?*
He/She/It's working.	*He/She/It isn't working.*	*Is he/she/it working?*	*Yes, he/she/it is.* *No, he/she/it isn't.*	*Where is he/she/it working?*
You/We/The're working.	*You/We/They aren't working.*	(2) ______ *you/ we/they working?*	*Yes, you/we/they are.* *No, you/we/they aren't.*	*Where* (4) ______ *you/we/they working?*

1 The present progressive is used with situations or events that …
a) happen all the time. **b)** are happening now or around now.
2 We form the present progressive with …
a) *be* + verb *–ing*. **b)** *be* + verb.

When the verb ends in e, drop the e before adding *-ing*: e.g., *take—tak**ing**, make—mak**ing**, live—liv**ing***

When the verb ends in consonant-vowel-consonant, double the final consonant: e.g., *plan—plan**ning**, get—get**ting**, stop—stop**ping***

C Practice **Complete these sentences with the present progressive form of the verbs in parentheses.**

1 Right now, I ______________ (*make*) a sandwich for lunch.
2 ______________ you ______________ (*have*) a good time?
3 What ______________ you ______________ (*do*) these days?
4 Sally ______________ (*not talk*) to me right now. I don't know why.
5 Come on! We ______________ (*wait*) for you!
6 Right now, Adele ______________ (*live*) in Montreal.

Watch out!
✔ Right now, I am studying.
✘ Right now, I am study.

D Now you do it **Work in pairs. Say what you think your friends and family are doing now.**

I think my best friend is buying me a present.

4 **Listening:** listening for numerical information

When you hear a number, think about the way it looks. This helps you understand what it is (e.g., a date, a time, a year, or a phone number). To help you remember a number, say it in your head when you are writing it down.

A Read these figures. Match them to what you think they refer to.

1 (301) 522-8801	**a)** a year
2 11/30/98	**b)** a time
3 12:52	**c)** a person's age
4 1998	**d)** a date
5 24	**e)** a phone number

How to say it

O can be said as both *zero* and *oh*

B Listen and repeat the numbers in Exercise A.

C Listen to these statements. Write the numbers you hear. Practice saying the numbers in English in your head when you are writing them down.

1 ____________ 4 ____________

2 ____________ 5 ____________

3 ____________

D Listen to three audio profiles from a high school reunion Web site. Complete the information below.

http://www.findfriends.com/home

home | register | help | login

Name: Danny Edwards

High school graduation year: (1) ____________

Date of class reunion: March (2) ____________

Name: Kathy Novak

Date of class reunion: August (3) ____________

Phone number: (4) ____________

Name: Candice Hughes

Reunion for year: (5) ____________

High school reunion at: (6) ____________ on: (7) ____________

Pronunciation: stressed verbs

5

A Listen to the conversations below. Notice how the speaker stresses the verb with *–ing* and not the verb *be*.

1 A: Where is the dog?
B: He's sitting on the sofa.

2 A: What are you doing?
B: I'm putting on my shoes.

3 A: Why are you stopping?
B: I'm tired.

B Work in pairs. Practice saying these conversations. Make sure you stress the correct verb. Listen and check. Then switch roles.

1 A: Is Mom at home?
B: No, she's swimming.

2 A: What do you want to do when you finish school?
B: I'm planning to get a Master's degree.

3 A: What's the score?
B: 3 – 4. Your team's winning.

4 A: Are you leaving?
B: Yes, I am. It's really late.

Language use: talking to an old friend

6

A Check (✓) the questions you could ask an old friend to find out about their life now.

B Work in pairs. You are old friends who meet on the street. Ask and answer the checked questions from Exercise A.

A: *Hi! How are you?*
B: *I'm fine! How about you?*
A: *I'm good, thanks. And how is your family?*

How to say it
Formal: *I'm fine.*
Informal: *I'm good.*

Unit 6

7 Vocabulary: a green lifestyle

A Amy has a very green lifestyle. Match the words and phrases to the pictures. Use the red boxes.

A

B

C

D

E

F

G

H

1 save water
2 turn off the lights
3 recycle
4 ride a bike to school/work
5 buy organic food
6 reuse bags
7 share a ride
8 clean up trash

B Do you have a green lifestyle? Check (✓) the things from Exercise A that you do to help the environment. Use the blue boxes.

C Work in groups. Ask your classmates questions to find out who has a green lifestyle. Make notes of your classmates' answers.

A: *Do you ride a bike to work?*
B: *No, I don't, but I share a ride. What about you?*

D Share the information with your classmates. Is anyone similar to Amy?

I think Irina has a green lifestyle. She rides a bike to school every day and she buys organic fruit and vegetables.

8 Grammar: present progressive vs. simple present

A **Language in context** Read this article about a veterinarian. Underline the "green" things he does at home and at work.

A "Green" lifestyle

Dr. Ralph Oliver **works** as a veterinarian at the San Diego Zoo. He **describes** his job—and his lifestyle—as "green": "I **want** to help the planet I live on." Oliver says that he **rides** his bike to work and **buys** organic food. At the zoo he **is doing** lots of things to help. "This month we **are saving** energy by turning off the lights in some areas at 7 p.m., not 8 p.m.," he says. "We also always **ask** visitors to clean up their trash. Even small things like this can make a big difference."

B Notice Look at the verbs in **bold** in Exercise A. Match the correct options to complete these sentences.

1 The verbs in the simple present describe … a) things happening right now or around now.
2 The verbs in the present progressive describe … b) things that are generally true or permanent situations.

We don't use the present progressive with some verbs:
e.g., *like, know, want, need*

C Practice Circle the correct options.

1 What *are you doing / do you do* right now?
2 Pete *is listening / listens* to his MP3 player right now.
3 I usually *have / am having* lunch around 1 p.m.
4 My cousin *wants / is wanting* to be a DJ when he finishes high school.
5 This food is delicious. I *am liking / like* it!
6 Right now, Mom *is taking / takes* a Spanish class.

Watch out!
✔ I want to help the planet I live on.
✘ I am wanting to help the planet I live on.

D Now you do it Write four sentences about your life in general and four sentences about your life right now. One of your sentences should be false. Read them to the class for them to guess which one is false.

Writing: writing simple sentences

9

Simple statements in English always have a subject and a verb, and often have an object, e.g.,
I *like* *cats and dogs.*
subject + verb + object
They usually appear in this order: subject – verb – object.

A Underline the subjects of the sentences and write *S*. Circle the verbs and write *V*. Underline the objects and write *O*.

1 I reuse plastic bags. (S V O)
2 People waste a lot of water.
3 Ian is reading an article about recycling.
4 We recycle all our paper.

B Write one sentence about each situation. Make sure you include a subject, verb, and object in the correct order.

1 ______________________

2 ______________________

3 ______________________

C Work in pairs. Compare your sentences. Correct any errors.

Self-direction and learning: making personal change

- Understand where you are now in your life.
- Decide what you want to change.
- Make an action plan.

A Check (✓) where you think you are right now on each chart.

I don't have a green lifestyle.

Being green

I have a very green lifestyle.

I always spend a lot of time alone.

Social relationships

I always spend a lot of time with friends.

I often have problems working/studying.

Work and study

I never have problems working/studying.

I have an unhealthy lifestyle.

Healthy living

I have a healthy lifestyle.

B Which area of your life do you want to change? Check (✓) one.

☐ Being green ☐ Social relationships ☐ Work and study ☐ Healthy living

C Write what you can do to make the change in Exercise B. Think of as many ideas as possible.

Social relationships
Cook dinner for my parents
Go to the movies with my friends

D Make an action plan. Write your ideas from Exercise C in the plan below.

MY ACTION PLAN

What area do you want to change?

___

What are you planning to do tomorrow to change your life?

___

What are you planning to do in the next month to change your life?

___

What are you planning to do in the next three months to change your life?

___

E Work in pairs. Share your action plan with your partner. Explain what you are planning to do. If you want to, ask questions about your partner's plan.

How to say it

Tomorrow, I want to ...

In the next month, I'm planning to ...

Reflect...

How can an action plan help you make changes in your life?

Language Wrap-up

p132–133

1 Vocabulary

A Read what people say about their lifestyles. Write the opposite of the adjective in bold. (4 points)

1 My lifestyle is pretty **healthy.** I exercise a lot and eat fruit. My boyfriend watches TV or plays video games all day. He has a very __________ lifestyle.

2 I work in an office every day. I guess my lifestyle is **boring.** My brother has a really __________ lifestyle. He's a police officer.

3 My sister has a really **relaxing** lifestyle. She studies in the morning and goes to the gym in the afternoon. Her husband has a very __________ life. He works from 8 a.m. to 9 p.m. every day, including Saturdays.

4 I try to be **green.** I recycle everything. My parents are really __________ , though. They throw out everything. They never recycle.

B Jerry is talking about his "green" lifestyle. Complete these sentences with words from the box. (6 points)

organic	lights	reuse	save	ride	share

"I try to have a green lifestyle. I (1) __________ water and I always turn off the (2) __________ before I go to bed. My office is pretty close to my apartment, so I usually (3) __________ my bike to work. Sometimes I (4) __________ a ride with a friend to go to the supermarket. I always buy (5) __________ fruit and vegetables and I always (6) __________ bags."

8–10 correct: I can talk about different lifestyles.
0–7 correct: Look again at Sections 1 and 7 on pages 58 and 62. **SCORE:** /10

2 Grammar

Read more of what Jerry says. Write the verbs in parentheses in the simple present or present progressive. (10 points)

"I (1) __________ (*not know*) why people are so wasteful. Right now, I (2) __________ (*read*) a great book about protecting the planet. More people should read it. Everyone (3) __________ (*know*) that traffic is a problem. It's obvious that people (4) __________ (*destroy*) the planet. Some people (5) __________ (*need*) to use a car sometimes, but not every day. Everyone should own a bike. I usually (6) __________ (*work*) downtown and I always (7) __________ (*ride*) my bike to work. Right now though, I (8) __________ (*work*) from home, so I don't need to travel anywhere! I know people (9) __________ (*not agree*) with everything I say, but now I think people (10) __________ (*learn*) that they should do more to protect the planet."

8–10 correct: I can contrast the simple present and the present progressive to talk about general time and what is happening now or around now.
0–7 correct: Look again at Sections 3 and 8 on pages 59 and 62. **SCORE:** /10

You Have Talent!

A Look at these pictures.
In your opinion, who is the most talented?

B Are you talented? Tell your classmates what talents you have.

A: Let's see ... I play the guitar. I speak Italian and French.

B: I think I'm talented. I play soccer.

1 Vocabulary: personality adjectives

A Match the positive qualities to the statements.

1 friendly	**a)** I'm happy. I think my life is great.
2 generous	**b)** I'm good at making plans.
3 patient	**c)** I usually do very well on exams.
4 reliable	**d)** I love buying things for other people.
5 optimistic	**e)** I never tell lies.
6 organized	**f)** I make friends easily.
7 smart	**g)** My friends can depend on me.
8 honest	**h)** I'm good at waiting for things.

B Work in pairs. Look at these pictures. Say what positive qualities from Exercise A you think these people have.

Bill Gates

Nelson Mandela

Angelina Jolie

I think Bill Gates is really smart because ...

C Work in pairs. Tell your partner which positive qualities from Exercise A you think you have and why.

I think I'm optimistic. I'm usually happy.

2 Language use: writing a reference

A Listen to this conversation. Complete the job reference for Carmen.

Job Reference for: *Carmen Dean* **Age: (1)** ______

Address: *12A Ocean Drive, San Diego, CA*

In my opinion, *Carmen* **is (2)** ______ **, (3)** ______

and (4) ______ **. He/She is ideal for the job**

of a/an (5) ______ **because of**

these qualities.

Referred by: *Jonathan Richards*

B Think about your best friend and their ideal job. Complete this job reference for them.

Job Reference for: ______________________ **Age: (1)** __________

In my opinion, __________ **is (2)** __________ **, (3)** __________ **and (4)** __________ **. He/She is ideal for the job of a/an (5)** __________ **because of these qualities.**

Referred by:

Reading: reading for the main idea p50 3

When you read for the main idea, look quickly at the text to find key words or phrases. These can tell you what the subject of each paragraph is. Key words are often nouns or adjectives.

A Look at the text below. What is it about?

Mystic Mavis says:

"**1** ______________

First of all, people born on February 29 are unlucky! They only have one birthday every four years! But because of this, they have special talents and abilities.

2 ______________

They are very friendly and optimistic. They always see the positive side of life. They are fun, and many of them can sing or dance very well. They have a lot of friends and they are always loyal to their friends.

3 ______________

People born on February 29 like their jobs and they want to be rich. But they don't usually give gifts because they aren't very generous!

4 ______________

These Pisceans usually have a healthy lifestyle. They eat lots of fruit and vegetables and they are good at sports."

B Look quickly at the paragraphs. Circle key words.

C Look at the key words you circled. Write these headings in the correct places in the text.

Health   Good qualities   Bad luck!   Work and money

D Read the paragraphs more carefully. Check your answers to Exercise C.

E Work in groups. Answer these questions.

1 Is anyone you know a February 29 Pisces? Do you agree with the text? Why or why not?
2 Do you read your horoscope? Do you think astrology influences our personality?

4 Grammar: *can/can't*—ability

A Language in context Match the pictures to what these people say about their pets.

1 ☐

2 ☐

3 ☐

http://www.pettalk.com/

Can your pet play a sport? Or sing? Or dance? Post comments about your pet's unusual talents below! The most talented pet will win a prize of $500!

a) Yes, he can. **My horse can play soccer!** He's really talented!
J.T. Williams, Texas

b) **My parrot can't talk, but he can draw.** He draws pictures with colored pencils!
Nina, Brazil

c) **Our dog, Muffin, can balance things** on his nose. It's very funny!
Mrs. Hill, Scotland

B Notice Look at the sentences in bold in Exercise A. Complete these rules with words from the box.

can't do can

1 We use ______________ to talk about ability.
2 *Cannot* is the long form of the word ______________ .
3 Questions and negatives do not use the auxiliary ______________ .

Affirmative	Negative	Questions	Short answers
It can fly.	*He can't play soccer.*	*Can they swim?*	*Yes, he can./No, he can't.*

C Practice Complete these sentences with *can* or *can't* and the correct form of the words in parentheses.

1 A: ___Can___ they ___play___ (*play*) tennis? B: Yes, ______________ .
2 Sally is a great chef. She ______________ (*cook*) French food.
3 I ______________ (*not open*) the door. Can you?
4 A: ______________ Angela ______________ (*speak*) Japanese? B: No, ______________ .
5 A: ______________ he ______________ (*play*) the guitar? B: Yes, ______________ .
6 We ______________ (*not hear*) the TV. Please turn down your music.

Watch out!
✔ She can dance.
✘ She can to dance.

D **Now you do it** **Work in pairs. Ask and answer questions about each other's abilities. Use the phrases below.**

• run a marathon • swim five kilometers • sing opera • dance salsa • play basketball

A: *Can you swim five kilometers?*
B: *No, I can't. Can you?*

Vocabulary: talents and abilities 5

A Complete these phrases with words from the box. Then check (✓) the things you can do.

can sing can play am good at can speak can cook can drive

1 I ________________ ☐ the guitar. ☐ the piano. ☐ chess.
2 I ________________ ☐ karate. ☐ salsa dancing. ☐ surfing.
3 I ________________ ☐ a car. ☐ a truck.
4 I ________________ ☐ a foreign language. ☐ Italian. ☐ many languages.
5 I ________________ ☐ opera. ☐ karaoke songs. ☐ traditional songs.
6 I ________________ ☐ French food. ☐ traditional dishes. ☐ healthy snacks.

B **Work in groups. Talk about the things you can and can't do.**

C **Tell the class about a talented person in your group.**

We think Emanuel is talented because he is good at salsa dancing, he can play chess, and …

Pronunciation: *can/can't* 6

A **Listen to the pronunciation of *can* and *can't* in these sentences. Notice that the vowel sound in *can* is weaker than in *can't*.**

1 I can speak French, but I can't cook French food.
2 I can't drive a car, but I can ride a bike.

B **Listen and repeat the sentences.**

1 My sister can dance, but she can't sing.
2 I can't speak German, but I can understand some words.
3 I can't ride a motorcycle, but I can drive a car.
4 I can hear you, but I can't see you!

7 Language use: listening to a review of a TV show

A Look at this picture. What kind of TV show is it? Do you have TV shows like this in your country?

B Listen to a man giving his opinion on the TV talent show *Dream Stars*. Circle the correct options.

1 There *are / aren't* dancers on the show.
2 The man thinks there *should / shouldn't* be more comics on *Dream Stars*.
3 *Dream Stars* is on TV *on the weekend / during the week*.
4 The man *likes / dislikes Dream Stars*.

C Work in pairs. Discuss these questions.

1 Which TV talent shows do you like? Why?
2 Which TV talent shows don't you like? Why not?

A: *I like American Idol because it's interesting.*
B: *Really? I don't like it. The contestants can't sing!*

8 Grammar: *can/can't* with adverbs of manner

A Language in context Read what a judge on a talent show thinks about one of the contestants. Is the judge's general impression of Shaliyah positive or negative?

Shaliyah is 24 years old, and she's from Jamaica. She's really friendly and talented. She can sing beautifully, but she isn't very organized. That's why she forgets the words to her songs sometimes. Also, she can't dance very well, but she learns quickly. I think we can help her with her dance steps. In my opinion, Shaliyah can win Dream Stars with a little help.

B Notice Read this information about adverbs of manner. Circle the adverbs in the text in Exercise A.

1 Adverbs of manner describe an action.
e.g., *She can sing* ***beautifully.***
2 Adverbs usually come after the verb.
e.g., *She can't dance* ***well.***

We usually form the adverb by adding *-ly* to the adjective:
e.g., *slow—slow**ly**, quick—quick**ly**, beautiful—beautiful**ly**, quiet—quiet**ly**, bad—bad**ly***

For adjectives that end in *-y*, we change the *-y* to *-i* and add *-ly:*
e.g., *funny—funn**ily**, noisy—nois**ily**, happy—happ**ily***

There are some irregular adverbs. Sometimes the adverb is different from the adjective, but sometimes it stays the same:
e.g., *good—**well**, fast—**fast***

Watch out!
✔ She can speak English well.
✘ She can speak English good.
✘ She can speak well English.

C Practice Rewrite these sentences with *can/can't*, the verbs in parentheses, and an appropriate adverb of manner.

1 Diane is a quick runner.
Diane ___can run quickly___ . (*run*)

2 Helen is good at French.
Helen ______________________ . (*speak*)

3 Paul isn't a fast swimmer.
Paul ______________________ . (*swim*)

4 Tom and Ellie are beautiful singers.
Tom and Ellie ______________________ . (*sing*)

5 You're a quiet worker.
You ______________________ . (*work*)

6 I'm not a good dancer.
I ______________________ . (*dance*)

D Now you do it Work in groups. Take turns talking about the things you can and can't do. Use the verbs and the adverbs of manner from the boxes.

drive	run	sing	speak	cook	dance	draw	paint

quickly	well	fast	beautifully

I can speak English well, but I can't run very fast.

Speaking: showing interest

9

You can show interest in different ways. One way is by using words such as *Wow!* and *How interesting!* The other is by using your face and your body.

A Look at these pictures. In which picture does the woman look interested?

1
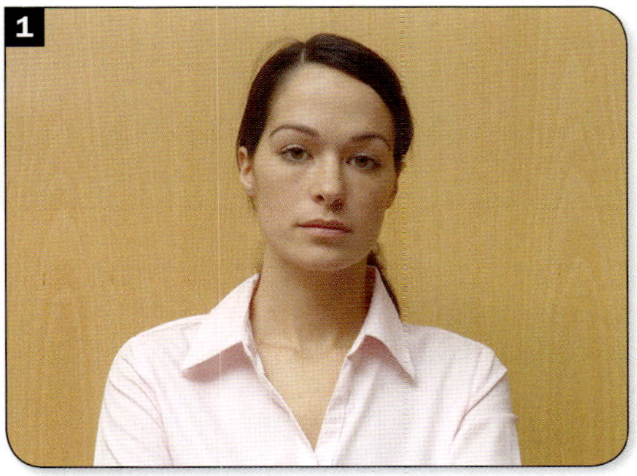

2

B Listen to the conversations below. Underline the expressions the people use to show they are interested.

1 A: So, what do you do?
B: I'm a pilot.
A: Really? That's amazing! Me, too!

2 A: Do you speak any other languages?
B: I can speak Chinese.
A: Wow! Really?

3 A: Can you cook Chinese food?
B: No, I can't, but I cook Indian food a lot.
A: Oh, how interesting!

C Listen to the expressions from Exercise B. Practice saying the expressions in an interested way.

D Work in pairs. Talk about things that your family members can do. Remember to use words to show interest.

A: *My sister is good at languages. She can speak Japanese, English, and Portuguese.*
B: *Wow, that's amazing!*

Collaboration:
working as a group to do a task

- Break up the big task into smaller tasks and make a list.
- Identify what the group can do together and what each person can do individually.
- Negotiate who can do any remaining tasks. Be flexible!

A Work in groups. Your school/university wants to have a talent show and they want your class to organize it. Add one or two things to each column in the to-do list below.

Logistics	*Participants*	*Promotion*	*Prizes*
Decide location.	*Decide on types of talent acts.*	*Design posters.*	______
Get permission to use location.	*Find judges.*	______	*Buy prizes.*
______	______	______	
Sell tickets.			

B Decide which tasks on the list the whole group can do. Write *G* (group) next to those things.

C Think about your preferences and abilities. Check (✓) the appropriate boxes on the survey.

http://www.workwithyourabilities.com/survey

Work with your abilities!

I prefer to work ...	◯ alone.	◯ with other people.
I can ...	◯ draw or paint.	◯ organize schedules.
	◯ do design.	◯ manage people.
	◯ write well.	◯ manage money.
	◯ talk to people easily.	◯ solve problems.

SUBMIT

D With your group, decide who can do each of the remaining things on your list.

A: *I can do design, so I can design the posters.*
B: *And I can paint, so maybe I can help you with the posters.*
A: *Yes, let's do them together.*
C: *OK, so you and Lisa can do the posters. What about the tickets?*

How to say it

You can ..., and I can ..., so maybe we can ... together.

I think you and Gina should ... because you can both ...

I can ... Should I ...?

What can you do?

I can ..., but I can't ...

OK, so why don't you ...?

Reflect...

How can breaking a large task into smaller parts make the task easier? Do you enjoy working with other people to do a task?

Language Wrap-up

1 Vocabulary

Complete this text with words from the box. (10 points)

patient	play	cook	honest	drive	sing	speak	generous	optimistic	smart

My mom is 52. She is very (1) ________________ and she buys a lot of gifts for me and my brother. She is really good in the kitchen. She can (2) ________________ delicious food. She is very (3) ________________ and never gets mad at my brother or me. She loves to go out with her friends and (4) ________________ karaoke. My dad is 54. He is a really good mathematician and he can (5) ________________ Italian and German, so I think he is very (6) ________________ . He can (7) ________________ the piano and the violin, too. My brother, Bruno, is 17. He really enjoys life and doesn't worry about the future, so I guess he is very (8) ________________ . He is (9) ________________ , too. He doesn't tell lies, and I know I can trust him. He is only 17, but he can (10) ________________ a car.

8–10 correct: I can talk about people's positive qualities and their abilities.
0–7 correct: Look again at Sections 1 and 5 on pages 68 and 71. **SCORE: /10**

2 Grammar

Write these words in the correct order. (10 points)

1 A: Francesca / dance / Can / well / ? ________________
B: can't / dance / No, / she / well ________________

2 A: sing / Can / you / ? ________________
B: beautifully / can / sing / I / Yes, ________________

3 A: Can / drive / well / David / ? ________________
B: drives / fast / No, / he / very ________________

4 A: Can / speak / you / a foreign language / ? ________________
B: speak / Yes, / I / English / well ________________

5 A: your / sister / swim / Can / fast / ? ________________
B: No, / fast / she / swim / can't ________________

8–10 correct: I can use *can*, *can't*, and adverbs of manner to talk about people's abilities.
0–7 correct: Look again at Sections 4 and 8 on pages 70 and 72. **SCORE: /10**

Shopping Around

Unit 8

A Look at these items. Check (✓) the things that you like to buy.

electronic equipment

food

clothes

accessories

furniture

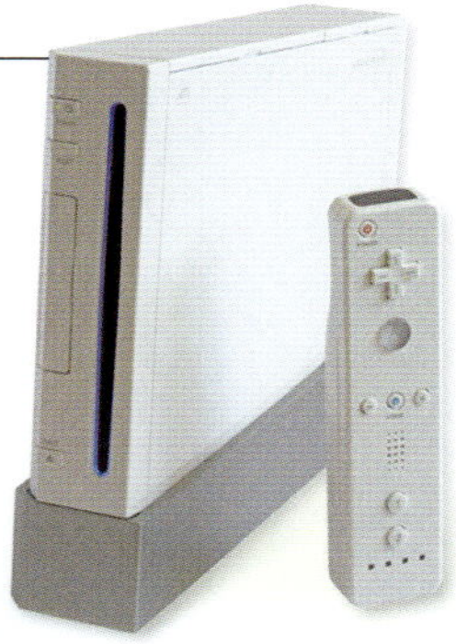

games

B Work in pairs. Talk about the different things you like and don't like to buy.

1 Vocabulary: clothes

A Match the words to the correct clothes in the picture.

1 a sweatshirt
2 a jacket
3 pants
4 sneakers
5 a dress
6 a suit
7 a skirt
8 a T-shirt
9 jeans
10 a shirt
11 a purse
12 a tie
13 boots
14 shoes
15 shorts

B Write the clothes in Exercise A in the correct column. Compare your answers in pairs.

Clothes I usually wear	Clothes I sometimes wear	Clothes I never wear

A: I usually wear jeans and a T-shirt.
B: Me, too. I never wear a suit …

2 Grammar: *this, that, these, those*

A **Language in context** Listen to the conversation below. Circle the clothes in the picture that Patty decides to wear.

Patty: What time is the party, Sasha?
Sasha: It starts at nine o'clock. I'm not sure what to wear. How about you?
Patty: I don't know. I want to wear my blue dress, but I think it's dirty.
Sasha: How about this skirt?
Patty: No, these jeans and that purple T-shirt are OK.
Sasha: What about shoes?
Patty: Oh, I want to wear those black shoes. I can't dance in them, but I love them!

B **Notice** Read the conversation in Exercise A again. Circle the correct options to complete the rules below.

1 We use *this/these* / *that/those* to talk about things that are close to the person who is speaking.

2 We use *this/these* / *that/those* to talk about things that are not very close to the person who is speaking.

3 We use *this/that* for *plural nouns* / *singular nouns.*

4 We use *these/those* for *plural nouns* / *singular nouns.*

C **Practice** Look at these pictures. Complete the sentences with *this, that, these, those.*

1 I really love ________ dress. I wear it all the time.

2 I'd like to wear ________ shorts to the beach today.

3 ________ is my favorite jacket.

4 I can't wear ________ shoes to the party. They're dirty.

D **Now you do it** Work in pairs. Look through the pages of your openMind book to find pictures of people. Ask and answer questions about the clothes they are wearing.

A: *Do you like those sneakers?*
B: *Yes, I do.*
A: *Do you like this T-shirt?*
B: *No, but I like that T-shirt.*

Watch out!

✔ I like these pants.
✘ I like this pants.

Language use: asking to try on clothes in a store

3

A Listen to this conversation in a clothing store. Match the assistant's questions to the customer's replies.

1 Can I help you?
2 Sure. Is it the right size?
3 Would you like to try a different size?
4 How is it?

a) No, it isn't. It's too small.
b) Yes, please. Can you get me a size 10?
c) Yes, please. I'd like to try on this jacket.
d) Fine. It fits perfectly.

B Make a list of clothes you need or want to buy in your notebook.

C Work in pairs. Student A, you are the assistant. Student B, you are the customer. Ask and answer questions about the clothes on your list in Exercise B. Then switch roles.

A: *Can I help you?*
B: *Yes, I'd like to try on these jeans.*
A: *Of course. Are they the right size?*

4 Listening: listening for numerical information p60

When you are listening to the price of something, try to write down the numbers as you hear them. You can then check the price by repeating it.

A Write each currency under the correct price. Then listen and repeat.

yen   cents   dollars   pounds   euros

1 ________ 2 ________ 3 ________ 4 ________ 5 ________

B Listen to these conversations. Match each conversation to the correct price.

Conversation 1:	**a)** €235,450
Conversation 2:	**b)** £17.68
Conversation 3:	**c)** $560
Conversation 4:	**d)** ¥999

C Work in pairs. Decide together how much each item below costs in dollars. Agree on a price and write it down.

$ ________

$ ________

$ ________

$ ________

D Listen to these ads for the items in Exercise C. Write their real cost. Are your guesses in Exercise C correct?

1 ________ 2 ________ 3 ________ 4 ________

How to say it

I think it costs about ...

I don't think so.

OK, let's say it costs ...

5 Language use: completing a survey

A Think about how often you buy these things. Discuss your habits with your classmates.

• clothes • books • CDs and DVDs • electronic equipment • cell phone cards

A: *I buy clothes every month.*

B: *Really? I buy clothes every week!*

B Read the survey on the next page. Answer the questions.

Phones Direct

CELL PHONE SURVEY

Thank you for agreeing to complete our survey. Please take about 5 minutes to answer the questions. Your answers can help improve our service.

Name: ______________ Age: ________ Male/Female: ________

How much do you usually spend on a new cell phone?

How often do you buy cell phone cards?

Every day ☐ Every week ☐ Every month ☐ Never. I pay a monthly bill. ☐

Where do you usually buy your cell phone cards?

Do you usually pay for your cell phone or cell phone cards ...

with cash? ☐ by credit card? ☐ by check? ☐

Do you ever buy cell phone cards online?

Yes ☐ No ☐

Thank you again for your time.

C **Work in pairs. Compare your survey answers. Discuss the differences or similarities in your shopping habits.**

A: *I buy cell phone cards every week.*
B: *Really? Well, I usually buy a cell phone card every month.*

Vocabulary: adjectives for describing gadgets 6

A Match the columns to complete these definitions.

When a gadget is ...

1 attractive	**a)** it is easy to use.
2 up-to-date	**b)** it doesn't cost a lot of money.
3 user-friendly	**c)** it is small.
4 compact	**d)** it costs a lot of money.
5 versatile	**e)** it can do lots of different things.
6 expensive	**f)** it can store a lot of information.
7 powerful	**g)** it looks good.
8 cheap	**h)** it is very modern.

B Read the conversation below. Complete the sentences with words from Exercise A.

A: Can you tell me about this cell phone?

B: Yes, sure. I love this cell phone because it's so easy to use—it really is (1) ______________ . And it's also (2) ______________ . You can go online and it has a digital camera.

A: Yeah, that's great. Is it (3) ______________ ?

B: No, it's actually very cheap ...

C **Work in pairs. Student A is an assistant in an electronics store. Student B is a customer. Ask and answer questions about the items below. Then switch roles.**

- MP3 player
- memory stick
- digital camera
- cell phone
- laptop

A: *Can you tell me about this laptop?*
B: *Yes, sure. It's versatile. It can do lots of different things.*

7 **Pronunciation:** emphasis with *this, that, these, those*

A Listen to the conversations below. Notice how we use stress to clarify information.

1 A: Is this my cell phone?
B: No, <u>that's</u> your cell phone.

2 A: Are these your bags?
B: No, <u>those</u> are my bags.

B Work in pairs. Practice these conversations. Listen and check.

1 A: Do you like this sofa?
B: No, but I like that one!

2 A: Do you want to buy these jeans?
B: No, I want to buy those jeans.

3 A: Do you have that CD?
B: No, but I have this CD.

8 **Grammar:** comparative adjectives

A Language in context Read this review. Circle the correct option to answer the question.

Are you looking for the perfect gift for Father's Day?

Then how about the new Ikon ZX8S digital camera? It looks cool and it takes fantastic pictures. It's cheaper than other digital cameras, too. The ZXTi, for example, is more expensive, but I don't think it takes very good pictures. It's also bigger and less compact than the ZX8S. The ZX8S is smaller, so it's better for vacations or traveling. It's more versatile than other cameras, and it's prettier. I'm giving the ZX8S 4.5 stars!

★★★★½ -Review by Ian Atkinson, Atlanta

Which camera does the reviewer prefer? **a)** the ZXTi camera **b)** the ZX8S camera

B Notice Read the review in Exercise A again. Complete these spelling rules for comparative adjectives.

One syllable adjectives	For most, add *-er: old—old**er**, smart—smart**er**, cheap*—(1) ___________ ↓ ***less** cold* For adjectives which end in consonant-vowel-consonant, double the final consonant and add *-er: thin—thin**ner**, hot—hot**ter**, big*—(2) ___________ ↓ ***less** hot* *This camera is smaller/bigger than that one.*
Two syllable adjectives ending in *-y*	Change the *y* to *i* and add *-er: happy—happ**ier**, funny—funn**ier**, pretty*—(3) ___________ ↓ ***less** happy* *His photo is funnier than her photo.*
Adjectives with two or more syllables	Use *more* or *less: interesting—**more** interesting, compact—↓ **less** compact, expensive*—(4) ___________ *The ZXTi is more expensive than the ZX8S.*
Irregular adjectives	*bad—worse, good*—(5) ___________ *Tom's camera is worse than this one.*

C Practice Complete these sentences with the correct comparative form of the adjective in parentheses + *than*.

1 This laptop is ______________________ (↑ *versatile*) mine.
2 Your furniture is ______________________ (↑ *nice*) your neighbors' furniture.
3 Shopping online is ______________________ (↑ *easy*) going to the store.
4 My cell phone is ______________________ (↓ *up-to-date*) yours.
5 These jeans are ______________________ (↑ *good*) those.
6 Mike's old MP3 player is ______________________ (↑ *big*) his new one.

Watch out!

✔ This TV is smaller than that one.

✘ This TV is more smaller than that one.

D Now you do it Work in pairs. Which of these two types of computer do you prefer and why?

- practical
- attractive
- compact
- cheap
- user-friendly
- good
- big

A: I like desktop computers because they're easy to use.
B: I don't. They're a lot bigger, and you can't carry them around.

Writing: writing compound sentences p63

9

We can use *and*, *or*, and *but* to connect two short sentences. This is called a compound sentence.
Use *and* to add extra information, use *but* to add contrasting information, and use *or* to show different options.
Use a comma before *and*, *but*, and *or*.

A Connect these sentences using *or*, *and*, or *but* in your notebook.

1 This furniture store is nice. It's expensive.
2 These pants are too ugly. They're too short.
3 Do you want to try on these shoes? Do you want to try on those shoes?
4 My computer is old. It's slow.
5 I like this cell phone. It's older than mine.
6 We can watch this movie. We can listen to that new CD.

B Choose gadgets (cell phone, radio, MP3 player, etc.) that you own. Write three compound sentences about them using *and*, *or*, and *but*.

1 ____
2 ____
3 ____

C Find someone in your class who owns similar items. Talk about why your gadgets are different.

A: My laptop is smaller than yours, and it's white.
B: Yes, but my laptop is more up-to-date.

lifeSkills

Thinking and problem-solving: making choices

- Understand the situation.
- Decide what your criteria are.
- Make a choice.

A Look at these pictures. Write the number of the picture next to the situation where you would wear clothes like this.

☐ a sports event
☐ a wedding
☐ a friend's party
☐ a school/university graduation
☐ the beach
☐ a job interview
☐ an English class

1

2

3

4

5

B Read this invitation. Circle the correct options.

Congratulations on your graduation!

We would like to invite you to attend this year's graduation ceremony on
Saturday June 23 at 7p.m.
in the Grand Auditorium.
Graduating students can bring a maximum of four guests with them to the ceremony.
Please wear evening clothes.

1 The situation is *formal / informal*.
2 You need to wear *special / ordinary clothes*.

C Work in pairs. Discuss the criteria below. Decide on two that are important to you when you buy clothes for a formal event.

- the type of event
- how much money you have
- the time of year (summer, winter, etc.)
- what your friends are wearing
- how fashionable the clothes are
- the store you shop in

A: *I think the time of year is important. Winter is colder than summer.*
B: *I agree.*

D Work in pairs. You are both going to the graduation and need to buy appropriate clothes. You each have a budget of $100. Choose from this online store.

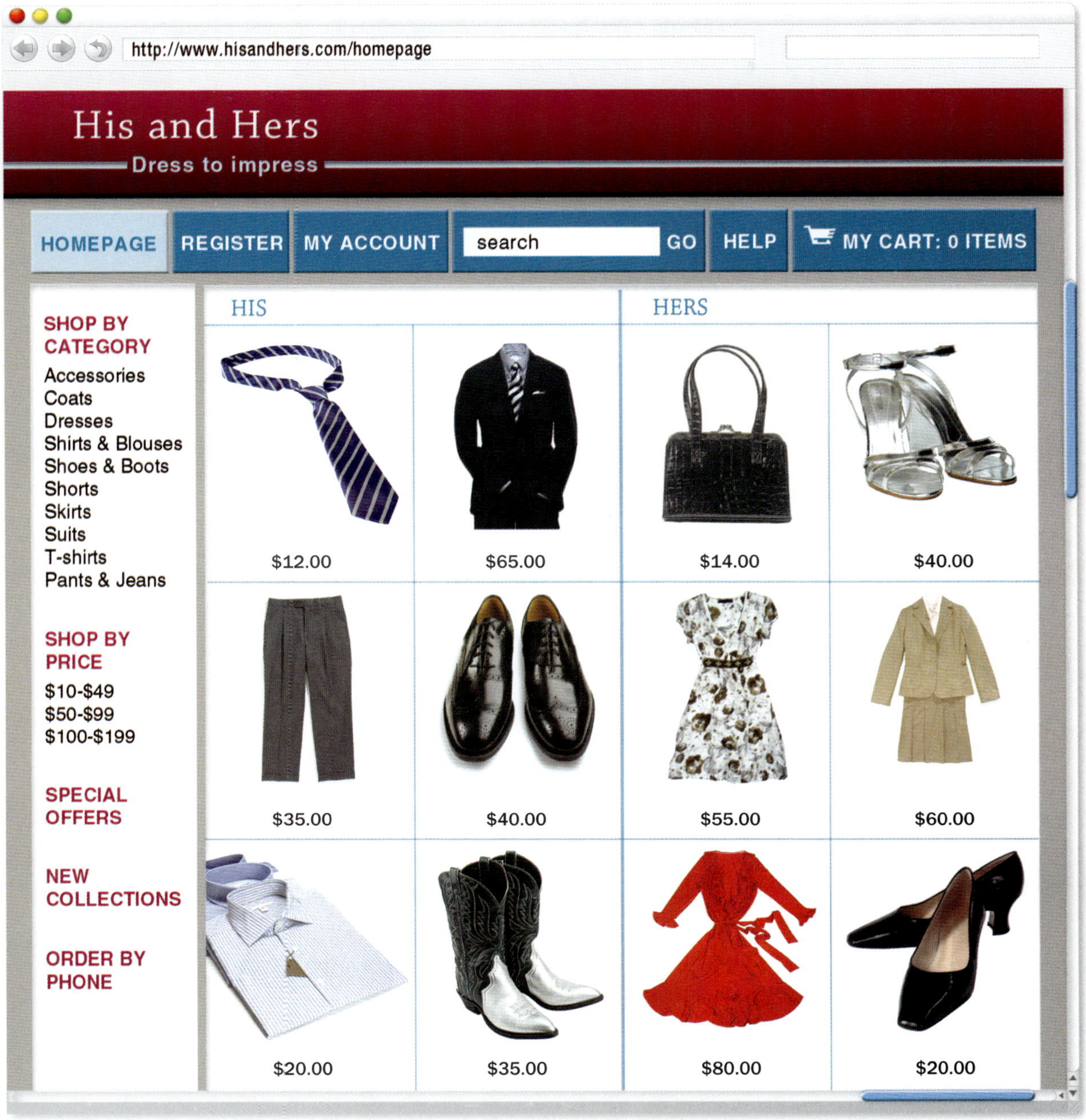

E Work in pairs. Talk about what you want to buy for the graduation and why.

How to say it

Evaluating:

I can't buy ... and ... because I only have $100.

I don't want ... because my graduation ceremony is in June.

... isn't very fashionable. I don't like it.

Making a choice:

I want to buy this ... because it's nicer than that one.

I'd like these ... They look really nice.

Those ... are good. And they're cheap.

Reflect...

How does having criteria help you make choices?

Language Wrap-up

p134–135

1 Vocabulary

A **Read the beginning of this e-mail. Write the clothing words in the correct blank. (5 points)**

1 
2 
3 
4 
5 

You should buy your sister clothes—a (1) ______________ or a pair of (2) ______________ that she can wear to the gym. Get your brother a cool (3) ______________ . Why don't you buy your mom a really nice (4) ______________ or a (5) ______________ ? Something she can wear in the summer.

B **Complete the rest of the e-mail with words from the box. (5 points)**

expensive
user-friendly
powerful
cheap
attractive

You can buy your dad a new cell phone. They're really (1) ______________ now. You can get a good one for only $60. Find one that's (2) ______________ . You know—nice to look at. Buy your grandmother a camera. Something (3) ______________ —she's not good with technology, so it needs to be simple to operate. You should buy your grandfather a telescope. He loves astronomy. You should get a (4) ______________ one so that he can see a long way. Be careful though—some telescopes can be very (5) ______________ —the best ones are over $700!

8–10 correct: I can talk about clothes and use adjectives to describe gadgets.
0–7 correct: Look again at Sections 1 and 6 on pages 78 and 81. **SCORE: /10**

2 Grammar

Read these conversations. Circle the correct options. Complete the sentences with the correct comparative form of the adjective in parentheses. (10 points)

1 A: Do you like (1) *this / these* shoes, Lisa?

B: Yes, but they're expensive. Look, those red ones are (2) ______________ (↑ *nice*) and they're (3) ______________ (↓ *expensive*), too.

2 A: Hi, Dana. Look at (4) *this / these* watch. It's a present from Tony.

B: Wow—I love it. It's (5) ______________ (↑ *good*) than my watch.

3 A: Hey, Tom. Do you know (6) *these / those* girls over there?

B: Yes, they're sisters. Erica is the taller one. She's (7) ______________ (↑ *pretty*) than her sister, Kate. Kate is (8) ______________ (↓ *easy*) to talk to. She's not very friendly.

4 A: Hey, Ann. Do you see (9) *that / those* man at the table? He's teaching our math class today.

B: Oh, good. I hope he's (10) ______________ (↑ *interesting*) than our regular teacher.

8–10 correct: I can use *this, that, these, those* to clarify what I am talking about and comparatives to compare things.
0–7 correct: Look again at Sections 2 and 8 on pages 78 and 82. **SCORE: /10**

Let's Eat

Unit 9

A Check (✓) the phrase that you most associate with food.

B Take a class survey. How many people chose each phrase as their number one association with food?

☐ an adventure

☐ a necessity

☐ a social activity

1 Vocabulary: food

A Write these food categories below. Guess the number of recommended servings per day for each category.

vegetables fat, salt, and sugar meat and other proteins fruit carbohydrates dairy products

1 Small quantities of

____

2 _______________

_____ servings per day

3 _______________

_____ servings per day

4 _______________

_____ servings per day

5 _______________

_____ servings per day

6 _______________

_____ servings per day

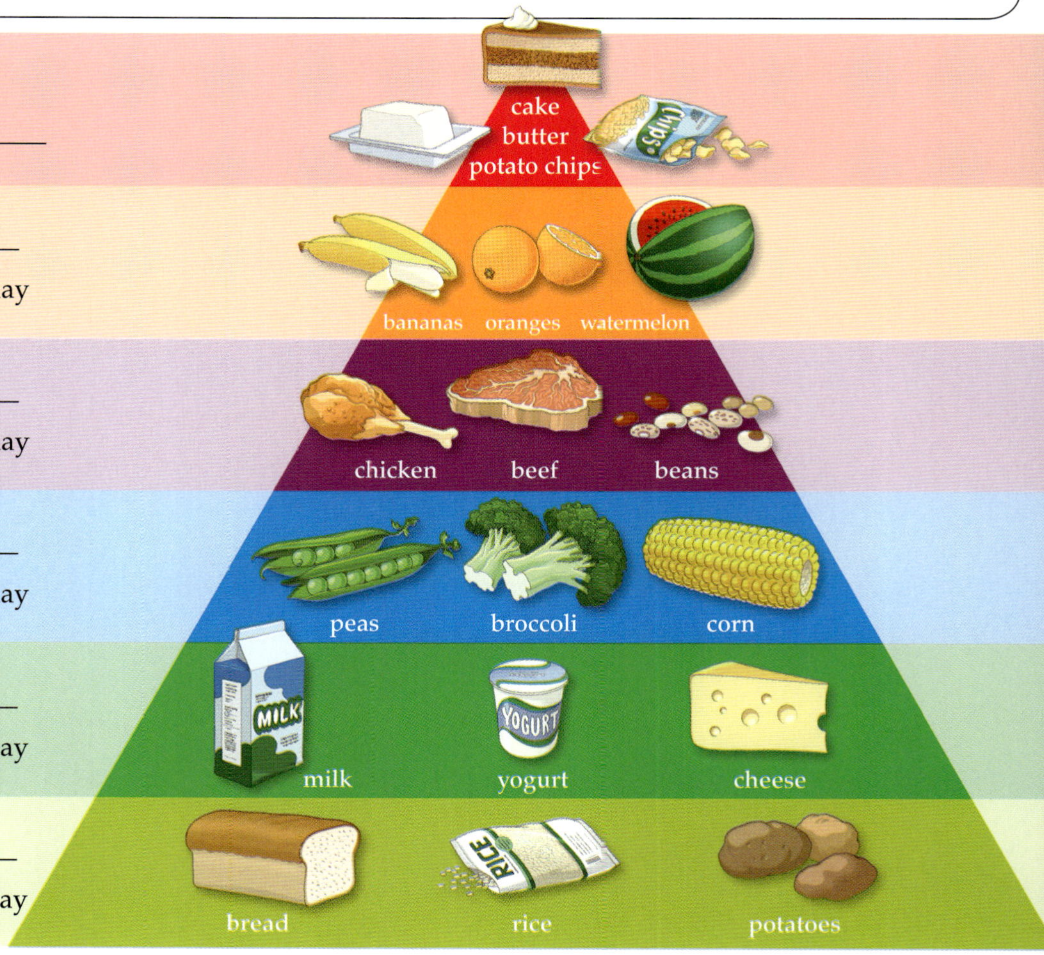

B Listen and check your answers to Exercise A.

C Work in groups. Talk about your diet. Who has the healthiest diet?

A: *Sandra, do you eat a lot of vegetables?*

B: *Not really, but I eat a lot of fruit. I love oranges and melon!*

2 Grammar: count and noncount nouns with *some, any*

A Language in context Read what these people want for lunch. Which lunch sounds good to you?

B **Notice** Read these rules. Write the foods from Exercise A in the example columns in the table.

1 Count nouns have singular and plural forms. Use *a/an* before singular count nouns.

2 Noncount nouns do not have a plural form. Do not use *a/an* before noncount nouns.

	Count nouns			Noncount nouns	
	Singular	Plural	Examples		Examples
Affirmative	*I want a banana.*	*I want some bananas.*	*chip—chips orange—oranges*	*I want some rice.*	*bread beef*
Negative	*I don't want a banana.*	*I don't want any bananas.*		*I don't want any rice.*	
Questions	*Do you want a banana?*	*Do you want some/any bananas?*		*Do you want some/any rice?*	

C **Practice** Circle the correct options.

1 Do you want *apple / an apple?*

2 I don't want any *cookie / cookies.*

3 Let's get some *banana / bananas.*

4 Do you like *onions / an onion?*

5 I want *a / some* rice with my steak.

6 We don't have any *vegetable / vegetables!*

7 Is there *any / an* ice cream in the fridge?

8 I don't like *beef / beefs.*

D **Now you do it** Work in groups. Discuss the kinds of food you usually have for lunch.

A: *I usually have meat and vegetables.*
I never eat any dessert.

B: *I usually have some soup and a sandwich.*

Language use: listening to and taking phone messages 3

A Read these messages. What is each message about?

1

While you were out
Caller: *Dan*
Day/Date: *Thurs, 2/04*
Time: *10:15*
Message: *lunch at John's Burgers, 2:30*

2

Ryan – message from Lauren
dinner Fri, 3/13. Call her.

B Listen to the two phone calls. Underline the incorrect information in each message in Exercise A.

C Listen to another phone call and write the message.

While you were out
Caller: *Ethan*
Day/Date: *Friday*
Time: *5:30*
Message:

4 **Speaking:** using phone language

A Listen to the two conversations below. Which is formal and which is informal?

1 A: Good afternoon, Food for Fun.
B: Hello. Could I speak to Ms. Linda Jenkins, please?
A: I'm sorry, she isn't here right now. Would you like to leave a message?
B: Yes. Please ask her to call Marsha Lind. My number is (640) 806-9271.
A: Yes, of course.
B: Thank you.
A: You're welcome.

2 A: Hello?
B: Hi, is Olivia there?
A: No, sorry, she isn't.
B: Oh, OK. Can I leave a message?
A: Sure.
B: This is Mark. Can you ask her to call me?
A: OK, no problem.
B: Thanks.

B Underline examples of formal and informal language in the conversations in Exercise A.

C Work in pairs. Follow the instructions below.

- Student A, "call" Student B and leave a message for another classmate. Student B, write down the message. Switch roles.
- Student A, "call" Student B and leave a message for your teacher. Student B, you are an office assistant at the school. Write down the message. Switch roles.

5 **Grammar:** verb phrases

A **Language in context** Listen to the conversation below. Why can't Jamie go out tonight?

Paul: So, would you like to go out to dinner tonight?
Jamie: Well, I'd love to, but I can't.
Paul: Why not?
Jamie: Because I have to study. I have a big math test tomorrow and I want to get a good grade.
Paul: Oh, too bad. Well, do you want to have dinner with me tomorrow night?
Jamie: Sure. Let's try that new Italian restaurant.
Paul: OK. I'd like to try it, too. I need to go to the gym first, so how about seven-thirty?
Jamie: Seven-thirty is fine. See you tomorrow.
Paul: OK, bye.

B **Notice** Look at this table. Underline examples of the structures in the conversation in Exercise A. Answer the questions below.

Statements for expressing desire	Questions for inviting	Statements of obligation/necessity
I would like/I'd like to … *I would love/I'd love to …* *I want to …*	*Would you like to …?* *Do you want to …?*	*I have to …* *I need to …*

1 What form of the verb is used after *would like, love, have, need, want?* **a)** infinitive (*to* + base form) **b)** base form

2 What word does the *'d* in *I'd* represent? ____________________

To make a suggestion use *Let's* + base form: e.g., ***Let's try*** *that new Italian restaurant.*

C Practice Complete this conversation with phrases from Exercise B. For some blanks, there is more than one correct answer.

Watch out!

✔ Would you like to go out tonight?

✘ Do you like to go out tonight?

David: Kayla, (1) ______________________ go to a movie tomorrow night?

Kayla: Oh, sorry. I (2) ______________________ , but I can't. I (3) ______________________ work. How about Friday night? I (4) ______________________ see that new Will Smith movie.

David: OK. Sounds good. And (5) ______________________ have dinner after the movie?

Kayla: Sure. (6) ______________________ have pizza?

David: Yeah, fine. Let's go to The Big Cheese.

D Now you do it Invite different classmates to do things. Accept or refuse their invitations. When you refuse, give a reason.

- have dinner
- go swimming
- go for coffee
- go shopping

A: *Would you like to go shopping tomorrow?*

B: *I'd love to, but I have to visit my grandparents.*

Vocabulary: ordering in a restaurant

6

A Complete this menu with words from the box.

pie chicken salad juice beef

The Laurel Tree

Appetizers

Shrimp cocktail	*$4.50*
Green ______________	*$3.95*
Tomato and onion salad	*$4.20*
Soup of the day	*$2.75*

Main courses

Fish (grilled or fried) with pasta	*$10.50*
Roast ______________	*$11.25*
Baked ______________	*$6.50*

Desserts

Apple ______________	*$3.75*
Strawberries & cream	*$3.25*

Beverages

Coffee	*$1.25*
Soft drinks	*$1.60*
Fruit ______________	*$2.75*
Bottled water (sparkling or still)	*$1.70*

B Listen to the conversation below. Are Jenny and Alan having lunch or dinner? How do you know?

Waiter: Good evening. Are you ready to order?

Jenny: Yes. I'd like the soup of the day first, please. And then I'd like the grilled fish.

Waiter: Sure. And for you, sir?

Alan: The roast beef, please, and a green salad.

Waiter: Vinaigrette, French, or Italian dressing?

Alan: Vinaigrette, please.

Waiter: Fine. And what would you like to drink?

Jenny: Just water for me.

Alan: And the same for me.

Waiter: OK. I'll be right back with your drinks.

C Work in groups. Role-play ordering in a restaurant. Use the menu above.

7 **Pronunciation:** weak *to*

A **Listen to the conversations below. Notice how *to* is weak in the first sentence and strong in the second.**

1 A: Do you want to watch a DVD?
B: I'd love to.

2 A: Would you like to go out tonight?
B: I'd like to, but I can't.

B **Work in pairs. Practice this conversation. Listen and check.**

A: Would you like to have dinner?
B: I'd like to, but I'm not hungry right now.
A: Do you want to go for a walk first?
B: Yes, I'd love to.

8 **Reading:** scanning for specific information

To find specific information in a text, don't read every word. Look at the text quickly to find the words or numbers that give you the information.

A **Read this situation. Underline the important information.**

You and your friends want to eat dinner late on Saturday because you are going to the theater first. You don't want to make a reservation. One of your friends is a strict vegetarian.

B **Scan this page of ads and find the best restaurant for the situation**

Amber

Fine international food in an intimate atmosphere
Extensive vegetarian menu

Hours Tuesday-Friday, 11:30 a.m.-11 p.m.
Saturday, 11:30 a.m.-1 a.m.
Closed Monday

Reservations required on weekends

Call (212) 452-0186
189 Congress Avenue

Brazil!

Traditional Brazilian barbecue
Huge salad bar

Open 6 p.m. to 11 p.m. daily
Reservations: (212) 456-9172

801 South Main St.

Bartlett's Bar and Grill

Steaks and seafood

Large variety of mixed drinks

Open daily from 11 a.m. to 9 p.m.

4701 Airport Boulevard
(212) 327-8854

Carlotta's Burgers

Steaks, burgers, pizza, and more

Try our specialty vegetable plates!

Live music
Friday & Saturday nights

Family-style seating

Hours:
Mon–Thurs, 11 a.m.–10 p.m.
Fri & Sat, 11 a.m.–2 a.m.

612 East Sixth St. • (212) 472-6643
No reservations necessary

C Read the ad for the restaurant you chose in Exercise B. Find this information as quickly as you can. Underline each item.

- the type of food
- entertainment
- the phone number
- the location

D Work in groups. Discuss these questions.

1 Do you prefer eating out or eating at home? Why?
2 What are your favorite kinds of restaurants?
3 What kinds of restaurants don't you like?

How to say it

I like vegetarian/steak/seafood restaurants.

I don't like noisy/quiet restaurants.

I prefer restaurants with traditional food/live music.

Language use: writing about a restaurant

9

A Read this blog. What two things does the writer like about the restaurant?

www.goodfoodblog.com

Good Food blog

Home | Login | Register | Help | Contact

Name: All That Jazz
Location: Barnes Road

All That Jazz is a New Orleans style restaurant and music club. The prices are a little high, but the food is excellent. Try the jumbo fried shrimp or the Cuban rice and beans. There is a very good jazz band on Friday and Saturday nights.

Posted by Michelle on July 3 Add comment E-mail

B Complete this information about a restaurant you like. Use your notes to write a blog entry in your notebook.

Name: ______________________

Location: ______________________

Type of restaurant: ______________________

Prices: Low ☐ Average ☐ High ☐

Recommended dishes: ______________________

Entertainment: yes / no

If yes, what: ______________________

C Work in groups. Read each other's blog entries. Discuss these questions.

1 Which of the restaurants in the blog entries do you know? Do you agree with the blog entry? Why or why not?
2 Which of the restaurants would you like to try? Why?
3 Can you recommend any other restaurants?

Organization and planning:
making a plan

- Make a list of the things you need to do.
- Write the things you need to do in a logical order.
- Add specific details to each thing on your list.

A **Work in groups. Look at these pictures of two styles of meals. Decide which style of meal you would like to prepare for a group meal and why.**

A

B

B **Work with your group. Number the steps for planning the meal in a logical order.**

☐ Decide what dishes to have. Include drinks and appetizers.
☐ Decide how much money you can spend.
☐ Decide what kind of meal you want (formal or informal).
☐ Decide when and where to have the meal.
☐ Check to see if anyone in the group doesn't eat certain foods.
☐ Make a shopping list. Include ingredients for the dishes and things you need apart from food, e.g., ice.
☐ On the day, get together to prepare your meal, and have fun!

How to say it

I'd like to prepare meal A/B because it's ...

more elegant/attractive/formal/informal/fun

easier/nicer

C Work with your group. Plan a meal for you and your group to have together. Complete this planning form.

How to say it

I think we can spend ...

Let's make/buy/have ...

How about steaks/ baked potatoes ...?

We need some/a/an ...

We need to ...

Planning the perfect meal

> An anniversary dinner for your parents? An informal lunch with friends? This form can help you organize a delicious and fun meal!

Part 1: The basics

Date of meal ______________________

Number of people (include yourself!) ____________

Location __________________________

Type of meal ☐ informal ☐ formal ☐ very formal

Budget $ ____________

Foods guests don't eat ______________________________________

____

____

Part 2: The details

Meal plan

> Appetizers

> Main course

> Dessert

> Beverages

Shopping list

> Food (include ingredients)

> Drinks

> Other things

D Work in groups. Make a copy of your meal plan on a piece of paper. Put your plan on the wall. Read the other groups' plans. Which meals would you like to be invited to?

Reflect...

What other types of activites can a written plan help you prepare for?

Language Wrap-up

1 Vocabulary

Complete this conversation with words from the box. (10 points)

green dessert shrimp sparkling soup cream pie bread fried salad

Waiter: Good evening. Are you ready to order?

Bruno: Yes. I'd like the (1) ______________ of the day to start and then the baked chicken.

Valerie: I'd like the (2) ______________ cocktail as an appetizer and then the fish.

Waiter: Would you like the fish grilled or (3) ______________ ?

Valerie: Um, grilled, please.

Waiter: OK. Would you like any (4) ______________ or vegetables?

Bruno: Yes, please. I'd like a (5) ______________ salad with some French dressing.

Valerie: And, I'd like potatoes and broccoli. We'd like a bottle of (6) ______________ water, too.

Bruno: Oh, and I'd like some (7) ______________ and butter, please.

Waiter: OK, thank you.

Bruno: So, do you think you'd like to have (8) ______________ later?

Valerie: Yes, I'd like to try some apple (9) ______________ or strawberries and (10) ______________ .

8–10 correct: I can talk about food and order food in a restaurant.
0–7 correct: Look again at Sections 1 and 6 on pages 88 and 91. **SCORE:** /10

2 Grammar

A Write the phrases from the box in the correct places in the e-mail. (5 points)

Do you want to bring I have to get up Would you like to come I need to go I'd like to cook

Hi Jill! How are you? I'm at work. (1) ______________ to my apartment for dinner tonight? (2) ______________ something really nice, and I don't want to eat alone! (3) ______________ something to drink and maybe some ice cream? We can watch a movie after dinner. I can't go to bed too late, though—(4) ______________ early tomorrow for a meeting. Anyway, (5) ______________ now. I have a lot to do. Call me later—hope to see you tonight. Love, Suzy

B Circle the correct options to complete Jill's answer. (5 points)

Sure. That sounds good, Suzy. I can bring some (1) *soft drink / soft drinks*. Do you like (2) *some strawberries / strawberries*? We can have strawberries with our (3) *ice cream / ice creams*. And how about (4) *a / some* cheese and (5) *cracker / crackers* before dinner? See you later. Jill

8–10 correct: I can use count and noncount nouns and verb phrases to talk about plans, invitations, and obligations.
0–7 correct: Look again at Sections 2 and 5 on pages 88 and 90. **SCORE:** /10

Speaking of the Past

A Check (✓) the pictures that represent your activities in the past month.

B **Count the boxes you checked and look at your score below. What is the average for your class?**

0–2 Are you bored? Try to have more fun!

3–4 A nice balance!

5–6 Whoa. Maybe you should relax a little!

1 **Grammar:** simple past—affirmative statements

A Language in context Read this tour evaluation. Answer the questions.

1 Were the Johnsons generally happy with the tour? 2 Were there any problems?

World Tour Service

Please take a few minutes to write a short evaluation of your tour with us.

We took a tour to Ireland, and we had a fantastic time. We especially liked Dublin. It's an amazing city! The tour guides explained everything very clearly, and they answered all of our questions. They knew a lot about Irish history. They were also very helpful, and they carried our heavy bags for us. The hotel in Cork was a little uncomfortable, but in general, we stayed in very nice hotels. We loved Ireland, and we'd like to go back.

Pam and Alan Johnson

B Notice Complete this table with simple past tense verb forms. Read the evaluation in Exercise A again. Check your answers.

Regular verbs		Irregular verbs	
Base form	**Simple past form**	**Base form**	**Simple past form**
answer	(1) ______	*be*	*was/* (7) ______
carry	(2) ______	*eat*	*ate*
explain	(3) ______	*go*	*went*
like	(4) ______	*have*	(8) ______
love	(5) ______	*know*	(9) ______
stay	(6) ______	*see*	*saw*
		take	(10) ______

Spelling rules for simple past regular verbs:
Most verbs: add *-ed (play—play**ed**)*
Verbs ending in *-e:* add *-d (prepare—prepare**d**)*
Verbs ending in consonant + *-y:* change *-y* to *-ied (stud**y**—stud**ied**)*

The verb *be* has two simple past forms:
I/he/she/it **was** and *you/we/they* **were**

C Practice Complete this e-mail with the simple past of the verbs in parentheses.

To: tracy_smith@mymail.com
From: robert_brown@mymail.com
Subject: The Grand Canyon

Hey, Tracy! Last week Susan and I (1) ______ (*go*) to the Grand Canyon in Arizona. It's incredible! The bus ride (2) ______ (*be*) tiring, but we (3) ______ (*be*) really happy when we arrived. We (4) ______ (*stay*) at a small hotel near the canyon, and the first evening we watched the sunset over the canyon. The next day we (5) ______ (*take*) a tour into the canyon. We (6) ______ (*see*) lots of birds and animals, and the guide (7) ______ (*explain*) the geology of the canyon. We (8) ______ (*have*) a great time on the trip!

D Now you do it Work in groups. Talk about the last trip you took.

My family/friends and I went to ... We stayed at ... It was ...

Pronunciation: –*ed* endings

2

A Listen to the verbs. Notice that the –*ed* endings are pronounced differently.

1 /d/ listened, played
2 /t/ liked, watched
3 /ɪd/ wanted, decided

B Listen and repeat the verb pairs.

want—wanted	practice—practiced
like—liked	hate—hated
end—ended	stay—stayed
work—worked	watch—watched

Language use: reading a survey

3

A Read the first paragraph of the article. What is the topic of the survey?

a) readers' birthdays b) readers' e-mail use c) readers' experiences

B Read and answer the survey.

It's Your Life e-mailed 100 readers on their birthdays and asked them how they felt about the past year of their lives. Then they completed a survey about specific positive experiences during the year. Many people were surprised at the results! For example, a lot of people who said, "It was OK," really had a fantastic year, according to the survey. Sometimes we focus too much on the bad or boring things in our lives! Now you try it …

My past year was … **a)** great. **b)** OK. **c)** not very good.

Now circle *yes* or *no* for each statement about your past year.

1	I took an interesting or fun trip.	yes	no
2	I went to some great parties.	yes	no
3	I met some new friends.	yes	no
4	I had a romantic relationship.	yes	no
5	I went out with my friends a lot.	yes	no
6	I did a lot of exercise or sports.	yes	no
7	I discovered some great music.	yes	no
8	I read some good books.	yes	no
9	I got a new pet.	yes	no
10	I learned a new hobby.	yes	no

Now look at your score. Every "yes" equals 1 point and every "no" equals 0 points. Does your general opinion of your past year match your score?

6 – 10—a great year!
3 – 5—an OK year
0 – 2—not a very good year

score

C Take a class survey. Answer these questions.

1 How many people in the class did each thing on the survey?
2 How many people had a great year?
3 How many people were surprised at the results?

4 Vocabulary: adjectives with *-ed* and *-ing*

A Read these examples. Answer the questions.

A: Do you think this movie is interesting?
B: No. It's boring.

A: Are you interested in this movie?
B: Not really. I'm kind of bored.

1 Which adjectives refer to the movie? What is the ending on the adjectives?
2 Which adjectives refer to the person who is watching the movie? What is the ending on the adjectives?

B Check that you know the meanings of the adjective pairs in the box. Then complete this letter with the correct forms of the words in parentheses.

interesting—interested	boring—bored	tiring—tired	exciting—excited	amazing—amazed

Hi, Joe & Sue,

We had a great weekend in New Orleans! It's an (1) ______________ (amaze) *city! We went to several jazz bars, and I loved them, but Sam isn't very* (2) ______________ (interest) *in jazz. Poor Sam—he was* (3) ______________ (bore)*! But we also went on a boat on the Mississippi River, and that was really* (4) ______________ (excite)*! We walked all around the historical district, and it was very* (5) ______________ (interest)*. We were pretty* (6) ______________ (tire) *on Sunday night, but it was fun.*

Love, Lynn

P.S. Here are a few pictures of New Orleans!

C Work in pairs. Talk about these things. Use *-ed* and *-ing* adjectives.

- the last movie you saw
- your last vacation
- the last sports event you saw

A: Last month I went to a baseball game. It was really exciting.
B: Really? I watched a soccer game on TV last night, but it was kind of boring.

Watch out!
The party was boring. =
✔ I was bored there!
✘ I was boring there!

5 Grammar: simple past—questions and negative statements

A Language in context Listen to the conversation below. Did Gary and Monica have fun on the weekend?

Gary: Hey, Monica. How was your weekend?
Monica: Terrible! I went camping with some friends, and I hate camping. I didn't have fun at all. Anyway, what about you? What did you do this weekend?
Gary: Oh, it wasn't very exciting. I didn't do much. Let's see, I watched TV on Friday night. On Saturday, I worked in the morning, and then I had lunch at Brennan's.
Monica: Really? Did you like Brennan's?
Gary: No, I didn't. The menu didn't have a very big selection, and the food wasn't very good.
Monica: And was it expensive?
Gary: Yes, it was!

B Notice Read the conversation in Exercise A again. Find the sentences in this table. Write the missing words in the table. Then circle the correct option to complete the rule below.

	be	Other verbs
Negative statements	*The food wasn't very good.*	*The menu* (4) ______ *have a very big selection.*
Yes/No questions	(1) ______ *it expensive?*	(5) ______ *you like Brennan's?*
Short answers	*Yes, it* (2) ______ *. / No, it wasn't.*	*Yes, I did. / No, I* (6) ______ .
Information questions	*How* (3) ______ *your weekend?*	*What* (7) ______ *you do this weekend?*

In negative statements, questions and short answers, use *did* or *didn't* with *be / other verbs.*

C Practice Complete these questions. Match them to the answers.

1 __Did__ you go out on Saturday night?
2 Where ______ you go?
3 ______ it fun?
4 Who ______ you go with?
5 What ______ you do on Sunday?
6 How ______ the food?

a) I went to lunch at Whole Earth.
b) To a club.
c) Yes, I did.
d) Excellent!
e) With my friends.
f) Yes, it was.

Watch out!
✔ What did you do on the weekend?
✘ What you did on the weekend?

D Now you do it Work in pairs. Ask about your partner's weekend.

A: *Did you go out on Friday?*
B: *No, I didn't. I stayed home and watched a DVD. What about you?*

Listening: understanding the main idea

6

It isn't necessary to understand every word of a conversation to understand the topic and the main idea. Listen for key words and repeated words.

A Listen to these conversations. Circle the topic of each one.

1 **a)** a vacation **b)** work **c)** the man's wife
2 **a)** a festival **b)** a trip **c)** the weekend

B Listen again. Circle the main idea of each conversation.

1 **a)** This person had a good time.
b) This person had a bad time.

2 **a)** This person had a good time.
b) This person had a bad time.

C What key words or repeated words did you hear? Listen again if necessary.

7

Writing: sequencing and connecting ideas

When we write or talk about an event, we usually tell the story in chronological order. We use specific words and phrases to indicate sequence.

A Read this blog entry. Answer the questions below.

http://www.supercoolpets.com/

Super cool pets blog

Home | Login | Register | Help | Contact

My dog, Joey

Two months ago, I found a dog in the street. First, I asked my neighbors if it was their dog, but it wasn't. Then, I made posters and put them around the neighborhood. Nobody called me.

After that, I put an ad in the newspaper. A week later, a man called, but it wasn't his dog. Finally, I decided to keep the dog. His name is Joey, and he's great!

Posted by Sarah on August 20

Add comment   E-mail

1 Which words indicate the order of events in the story?
2 What punctuation do we use after sequencing words at the beginning of a sentence?

B Number the sentences in a logical order to form a story. There is more than one correct order!

☐ … ago, I had an amazing day!

☐ She had tickets for the U2 concert that night! The concert was amazing.

☐ … she really surprised me!

☐ It was my birthday, and my girlfriend picked me up at my house in the afternoon.

☐ … we went home at about midnight. It was really an incredible birthday!

☐ … we went shopping. She bought me some CDs and a jacket.

☐ … she took me to a really nice restaurant for lunch.

C Write the story in your notebook. Add sequencing words and time expressions where indicated.

D Work in pairs. Read your stories. Are they exactly the same? If not, are they both logical?

Vocabulary: memorable experiences

8

A Write sentences that are true for you using the ideas below. Add more information.

... ago,		saw	a famous person. an amazing concert.
Once	I	took	a trip to ... a picture of ...
Last ... ,		got	a special letter. a fantastic gift.

B Work in groups. Compare your sentences.

A: *Once I saw a famous person. I saw George Clooney at the airport.*
B: *Really? Wow!*

Language use: talking about an experience

9

A Listen to the conversation below. Did Sally have a good experience or a bad experience?

Sally: I was on TV three months ago.
Ann: Really? What show were you on?
Sally: My boyfriend and I were on *Dance Craze.*
Gary: Wow! Did you win?
Sally: Yes, we did! We won two hundred dollars.
Ann: Really? That's amazing!

B Think of an experience that happened to you. Write notes.

The experience: ______________________

____

When it happened: ______________________

Where it happened: ______________________

Other information: ______________________

____

Time expressions:
yesterday
last Tuesday/week/month/year
three hours/days/weeks/months/years ago
in March/2010

C Work in groups. Talk about your experience. Answer any questions from people in your group.

Information and research: taking notes on a text

- Read the text to understand the main idea. Don't take notes.
- Read the text again. Underline the important information.
- Write key words and phrases in your notebook. Don't copy complete sentences.
- Reread your notes. Are they logical? Do they help you remember what you read?

A Read this text. Why is the culture of New Orleans different from the culture in other parts of the U.S.?

New Orleans, a City with a Different Flavor

The biggest cultural influence in the U.S. is from Great Britain, but one exception to that is in New Orleans, on the Mississippi River. In the 17th Century, the French explorer LaSalle claimed the river for France, and in 1718, the French founded New Orleans. The city became a favorite port for pirates! In 1762, France ceded New Orleans to Spain, but in 1800, Spain returned the city to France. Finally, in 1803, France sold the territory, including New Orleans, to the U.S.

Many Americans went to live in New Orleans, but French speakers continued to dominate in the 19th and early 20th Centuries. They did not come only from France, but also from Haiti (a former French possession) and from Canada. The French-speaking Canadian immigrants were Acadians (called Cajuns). The French, the Cajun, and the Haitian cultures joined together to create the unique architecture, cuisine, and music that are famous in New Orleans today.

B Read the text again. Underline information that relates to this question: What is the history of French speakers in New Orleans?

C Read these notes. Compare the information in the notes with the information you underlined. Is it the same?

The history of French speakers in New Orleans

17th Century—LaSalle claimed Mississippi River for France
1718—French founded N.O.
1762—French gave N.O. to Spain
1800—Spain returned N.O. to France
1803—France sold N.O. to U.S.
19th & 20th Centuries: French speakers from France, Haiti, Canada (Cajuns) created unique architecture, cuisine, and music

D **Work in pairs. Student A, read the question about Dubai and read the text. Student B, read the question about Hong Kong and read the text.**

Question: How did Dubai become a wealthy city?

Dubai for Business

Dubai, on the Arabian Gulf, is an important international center of finance and tourism. Many people think that Dubai's success is only because of its petroleum, but petroleum is only one factor. In the 19th Century, Dubai became a major port and center of commerce on shipping routes from India. It also had an enormous international market for its pearls. Dubai was already a wealthy city, and the discovery of oil in 1966 made it much, much wealthier.

Sheikh Rashid, Dubai's leader since 1958, used oil money to modernize the infrastructure of Dubai. He made Dubai a free port, and it became the major business center for the region. Rashid also promoted Dubai as a tourist destination. In the 1970s, Dubai joined with six other emirates to form the United Arab Emirates. The UAE is now one of the richest nations in the world.

Question: What was the role of Great Britain in the history of Hong Kong?

The British in Hong Kong

Before the 19th Century, the island of Hong Kong had a very small population. The residents were Chinese fishermen (and a number of pirates!). In 1842, Britain defeated China in a war and took possession of the island of Hong Kong. (The island gets its name from the abundance of flowers that grow there. "Hong Kong" means "fragrant flower.") In a second war, Britain got Kowloon, across the harbor from Hong Kong. Finally, in 1898, a large area next to Kowloon also became British property. This annexation gave the British more space to expand the colony.

Britain established a major port in Hong Kong, and the city became famous for shipping, banking, and insurance. Many people immigrated to Hong Kong from China in the 20th Century. In 1984, Britain agreed to return Hong Kong to China in 1997. On July 1, 1997, in a big celebration, it officially became part of China. Today Hong Kong is still one of the world's major financial centers.

E **Read your text again and underline information that relates to the question.**

F **Use the underlined information in your text to write notes in your notebook. Reread your notes to check that you can understand them.**

G **Close your book. Use your notes to tell your partner about the text you read.**

How to say it

My text was about ..., and my question was ...
The history of the city began in ...
The first residents were [nationality].
It became ...

Reflect...

Taking notes helps you study more efficiently. Look at your notes for other classes. Can you improve them?

Language Wrap-up

p136–137

1 Vocabulary

Complete these sentences with phrases from the box. Circle the correct options. (10 points)

saw a concert	met a famous person	got a special letter	took a trip	got a fantastic gift

I had a great weekend. My friend and I (1) ______________________ to Niagara Falls. It was pretty (2) *amazed / amazing*.

It was my birthday yesterday. I (3) ______________________ from my parents. They gave me a digital camera. I was really (4) *excited / exciting*.

My husband (5) ______________________ in the mail yesterday. It was an invitation to meet the President. He was really (6) *surprised / surprising*.

I had a great weekend. I (7) ______________________ on Saturday night. Manu Chao played in Detroit. The trip was pretty (8) *tired / tiring*, but it was a fantastic night!

I (9) ______________________ once. He is a famous movie director. He sat next to me on a flight to New York. We talked a lot about movies. He was very (10) *interested / interesting*.

8–10 correct: I can talk about memorable experiences and use adjectives with *-ed* and *-ing* endings.
0–7 correct: Look again at Sections 4 and 8 on pages 100 and 103. **SCORE: /10**

2 Grammar

Complete this postcard with the correct simple past form of the verbs in parentheses. (10 points)

To: jasminep@mymail.com
From: louisa_scott@mymail.com
Subject: New York!

Hi Jasmine,
Here I am in New York. It's great. The hotel is amazing and the people are really friendly. When I (1) ______________ (*arrive*) at the airport, I (2) ______________ (*take*) a taxi to the hotel. The views from the Queensboro Bridge (3) ______________ (*be*) spectacular. Then I (4) ______________ (*meet*) my friend Amy, and we (5) ______________ (*go*) out for dinner and (6) ______________ (*have*) a pizza—it was really delicious! I (7) ______________ (*not stay*) out too late, though. I (8) ______________ (*be*) really tired. And how are you? What (9) ______________ you ______________ (*do*) to celebrate your birthday?
Sorry I (10) ______________ there!
Louisa

8–10 correct: I can use the simple past to talk about past events and to ask questions about past events.
0–7 correct: Look again at Sections 1 and 5 on pages 98 and 100. **SCORE: /10**

Great Lives

Unit 11

A How many of these people do you recognize? What were their occupations?

Luciano Pavarotti

Selena Quintanilla

Indira Gandhi

Evel Knievel

John F. Kennedy

Julius Caesar

Florence Griffith-Joyner

B Work in pairs. Put the people in Exercise A in different groups or pairs according to their similarities. Think of as many combinations as possible.

A: *Evel Knievel and Florence Griffith-Joyner were both sports stars.*

B: *J.F.K. and Evel Knievel were both from the U.S.*

1 **Reading:** scanning for specific information p92

A **Work in pairs. Student A, scan the first paragraph and complete sentences 1–5. Student B, scan the second paragraph and complete sentences 6–10.**

Seabiscuit

The story of the racehorse Seabiscuit is a story about starting at the bottom and finishing at the top. Seabiscuit was born in Kentucky on May 23, 1933, during the Great Depression. He wasn't a beautiful horse, and he was small for a racehorse. In his first two years, he wasn't very good, and he didn't win many races. Then, in 1936, his owner sold him to Charles Howard, an automobile salesman. Howard moved Seabiscuit to his ranch in California, and the legend began.

With trainer Tom Smith and jockey Red Pollard, Seabiscuit began to win races. Seabiscuit and his owner, Charles Howard, were favorites with the press and with the American people. Seabiscuit had one especially incredible achievement in his career. In 1938, he beat War Admiral, the number one racehorse in the country. He retired in 1940, and he died on May 17, 1947. To the millions of poor people during the Depression, Seabiscuit symbolized hope for the "little guy."

Tobey Maguire in the movie *Seabiscuit*

Student A

1 Seabiscuit was born in (place) ______________________ .

2 Seabiscuit was born on (date) ______________________ .

3 Charles Howard bought Seabiscuit in (year) ______________________ .

4 Howard was a (job) ______________________ .

5 Howard's ranch was in (place) ______________________ .

Student B

6 Seabiscuit's trainer was named ______________________ .

7 Seabiscuit's jockey was named ______________________ .

8 Seabiscuit beat War Admiral in (year) ______________________ .

9 Seabiscuit retired in (year) ______________________ .

10 Seabiscuit died in (year) ______________________ .

B **Ask your partner questions to complete the sentences for the other paragraph.**

A: *Where was Seabiscuit born?*

B: *In Kentucky. What was the trainer's name?*

C **Read both paragraphs more carefully. Check your sentences for errors.**

D **What other real or fictional animal or human heroes do you know? What did they do?**

Grammar: simple past with *when* clauses

A Language in context **Read this article. Why do people remember Steve Irwin?**

The Real Crocodile Hunter

Steve Irwin was a famous conservationist and TV show host. He was born in Australia in 1962, and he grew up on his parents' wildlife park. Steve loved reptiles, and he got a python for his birthday when he was six years old! When Steve was older, he learned to work with crocodiles. In 1996, Irwin started his TV show, *The Crocodile Hunter*, and it became popular in many countries. On September 4, 2006, when Steve went to the Great Barrier Reef to film ocean animals, a stingray stung him. He died that day of cardiac arrest. **People all over the world were sad when Steve Irwin died.** Many people still remember his excellent work.

B Notice **Read the sentence in bold in the text in Exercise A. Circle the correct options.**

1 Which action happened first?

a) People were sad. **b)** Steve Irwin died.

2 The action in the *when* clause happened … the other event in the sentence.

a) at the same time or before **b)** after

When clauses can go at the beginning or at the end of a sentence:

e.g., ***When*** *Steve was older, he learned to work with crocodiles.* (Use a comma.)

Steve learned to work with crocodiles ***when*** *he was older.* (Don't use a comma.)

C Practice **Rewrite these sentences, changing the position of the *when* clause.**

1 When my friend told me the news, I was surprised.

I was surprised when my friend told me the news.

2 Sally was happy when she got a new car.

____

3 I got a puppy when I was ten.

____

4 When I was little, I loved going to the movies.

____

5 People were surprised when the horse won the race.

____

6 When I went shopping, I saw my teacher.

____

7 When our friends arrived, my roomate was asleep.

____

D Now you do it **Work in groups. Tell your group about the things below.**

- something that happened when you were young
- something you loved when you were little
- something that happened the last time you went out

I forgot my I.D. card when I went out last Friday. I couldn't go dancing.

3 **Vocabulary:** life events

A Write the phrases from the box under the pictures.

retire	graduate	have children	get a job

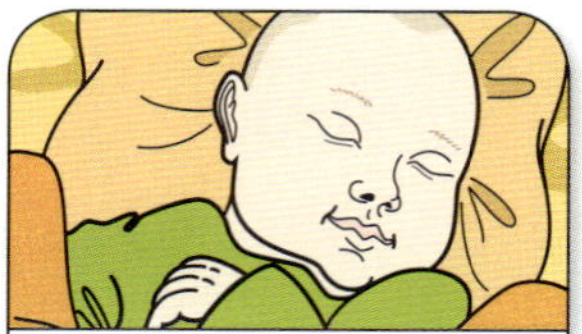

1 be born

2 grow up

3 ______________

4 ______________

5 get married

6 ______________

7 ______________

8 die

B Listen and check your answers to Exercise A.

C Work in pairs. Tell your partner about a family member's life. Use as many of the expressions in Exercise A as you can.

My grandfather was born in 1940. He grew up in a small town. He graduated from high school in 1958 …

4 **Language use:** listening to a life story

A Read these notes. Then listen to the life story. Do not try to complete the notes yet.

Florence Griffith–Joyner (Flo Jo)

Place of birth:
Date of birth:
First Olympic competition: Los Angeles, 1984
Silver medal in the ______ *meter race*
Also famous for: long, painted fingernails and colorful ______
Country of 1988 Olympics:
Number of gold medals:
Year she retired:
Date she died:

B Listen again and complete the notes in Exercise A.

C What other interesting or surprising facts did you learn about Florence Griffith-Joyner?

Speaking: taking time to think 5

Sometimes we need time to think of the answer to a question, or we need to think about the language to use. We use certain words and phrases to give us time to think.

A Listen to the conversation below. Underline the words and phrases the speakers use to take time to think.

Alison: What were the names of all The Beatles?
Jenny: Uh, I can't remember.
Chris: Let me think. Oh, yeah. Their names were John, Paul, George, and Ringo.
Alison: That's right. And when did George die?
Jenny: Just a second. I'm not sure, but I think he died in 2001.
Chris: Did your parents like The Beatles?
Alison: Well, my dad did, but my mom didn't like them very much.

B Work in groups. Do the quiz together. Take time to think before answering if necessary.

BLAST FROM THE PAST TRIVIA QUIZ

Two points per correct answer

1. What famous tenor died in 2007?
2. Who was the male star in *Titanic*?
3. Where was Jennifer Lopez born?
4. Who was Heath Ledger?
5. In what city did John Lennon die?
6. What famous book did Mary Shelley write?
7. Who was the "King of Pop"?
8. Where did the character Harry Potter go to school?
9. What company sold about 140 million MP3 players from 2001 to 2008?
10. What nationality was Indira Gandhi?

1 Luciano Pavarotti 2 Leonardo diCaprio 3 New York 4 An actor (from Australia, died in 2008) 5 New York 6 Frankenstein 7 Michael Jackson 8 Hogwarts School of Witchcraft and Wizardry 9 Apple® 10 Indian

C Check your answers and calculate your score. Which group is the winner?

6 **Grammar:** object pronouns

A Language in context **Read this text. How many Nobel prizes did Marie Curie win?**

A young woman, Maria Sklodowska, went from Poland to Paris in 1891 to study at the Sorbonne. Pierre Curie was a lab director at the university. Maria (now called Marie) met **him** there and they fell in love. She married **him** in 1895 and they began to work together. In 1898, they discovered polonium and radium. In 1903, the Swedish Academy gave **them** a Nobel prize for their discovery of radioactivity. When Pierre Curie died, Marie continued their work. The academy gave **her** a second Nobel Prize in 1911 for her work in chemistry.

B Notice **Look back at the text in Exercise A. Who or what do the pronouns in bold refer to? Complete the table.**

Subject	Object
I	*me*
you	*you*
he	(1) ______
she	(2) ______
it	*it*
we	*us*
you	*you*
they	(3) ______

Watch out!
✔ She met him.
✘ She met to him.

C Practice **Replace the underlined words with pronouns.**

1 My father fell in love with my mother when he met my mother.
2 I met my best friends, David and Lisa, at a party. I met David and Lisa five years ago.
3 I gave my brother an MP3 player. I gave my brother the player for his birthday.
4 My sister and I gave my mother some chocolate for Valentine's Day. She loved the chocolate!
5 My parents gave my wife and me a great Christmas gift. They gave my wife and me a new car!
6 It was my daughter's birthday yesterday. I took my daughter out to dinner.

D Now you do it **Work in groups. Ask and answer these questions.**

1 Who is your best friend? When did you meet him/her?
2 What was the last present someone gave you? Did you like it? Why or why not?
3 When was the last time you went out with your friends? Where did you go?

7 **Pronunciation:** object pronouns

A **Listen to these sentences. Notice that object pronouns are not usually stressed.**

1 I met David and Lisa at a party.
I met them at a party.

2 I saw my teacher at the mall.
I saw him at the mall.

B **Work in pairs. Practice saying these sentences. Then listen and check.**

1 My mom loved The Beatles.
My mom loved them.

2 I gave my brother an MP3 player.
I gave him an MP3 player.

3 Cervantes wrote *Don Quixote* in 1605.
Cervantes wrote it in 1605.

Vocabulary: historical events

8

A **Complete these sentences about historical events with words from the box.**

won	built	invented	explored	wrote	fought	composed	discovered

1 The U.S. ____________ its independence from England in 1783.

2 Marco Polo ____________ China for the first time in 1271.

3 Gustave Eiffel ____________ the Eiffel Tower in 1889.

4 The Egyptians ____________ cosmetics in 4,000 B.C.

5 Anton van Leeuwenhoek ____________ bacteria in 1683.

6 Cervantes ____________ *Don Quixote* in 1605.

7 Napoleon ____________ the Battle of Waterloo in 1815.

8 Georges Bizet ____________ the opera *Carmen* in 1875.

B **Listen and check your answers to Exercise A.**

C **Write a history question using one of the verbs in Exercise A. Ask your classmates the question.**

A: *Who wrote Hamlet?*

B: *Shakespeare wrote it.*

Watch out!

✔ Who invented the radio?

✘ Who did invent the radio?

Language use: writing a short biography

9

A **Read this biographical information about Ray Tomlinson.**

Modern inventors Ray Tomlinson

Ray Tomlinson invented one of the most important things in the computer world—electronic mail, or e-mail. Tomlinson was born in Amsterdam, New York, in 1941. He graduated from the Massachusetts Institute of Technology with a Master's Degree in electrical engineering in 1965. Two years later, he got a job at a technology company. In 1971, Tomlinson wrote a program to send electronic mail between different computers.

Tomlinson used the symbol @ to separate the user from the computer, and we still use that symbol today. We express the symbol as *at*.

B **Use the fact file below to write a similar biography of Tim Berners-Lee.**

Tim Berners-Lee

Achievement: invented the World Wide Web

Born: London, England, June 8, 1955

University: graduated from Oxford University in 1976

First job after graduation: at a telecommunications company, as a programmer (1976)

Year he invented the World Wide Web: 1990

Year the Web started on the Internet: 1991

C **Work in groups. Make a list of ten people in history. Read your list to the class and say what each person did.**

William Shakespeare wrote many famous plays.

Collaboration:
brainstorming in a group

- Brainstorm (think of ideas) by yourself.
- Brainstorm with other people. Combine your ideas.
- Choose and develop the best idea or ideas.

A **Read about the project. Brainstorm by yourself. In your notebook, write as many names in each category of the table below as you can.**

Here is your project ...

You have to choose one person to include in a Web site about great lives. Follow these guidelines.

- The person should be from your country.
- The person can be alive or dead.
- The person should have at least one big achievement in his/her life.

Great Lives			
Politics	Entertainment	The arts	Sports

B **Work in groups. Make a combined list of great lives. What do you notice about the combined list compared to your personal list?**

How to say it

I think ... is good because (s)he is/was a very famous ...

Do you know a lot about him/her?

What are/were his/her achievements?

I prefer ... because ...

C With your group, look at your combined list. Choose one person from the list to write a web entry about.

D With your group, complete as much of the word web as you can.

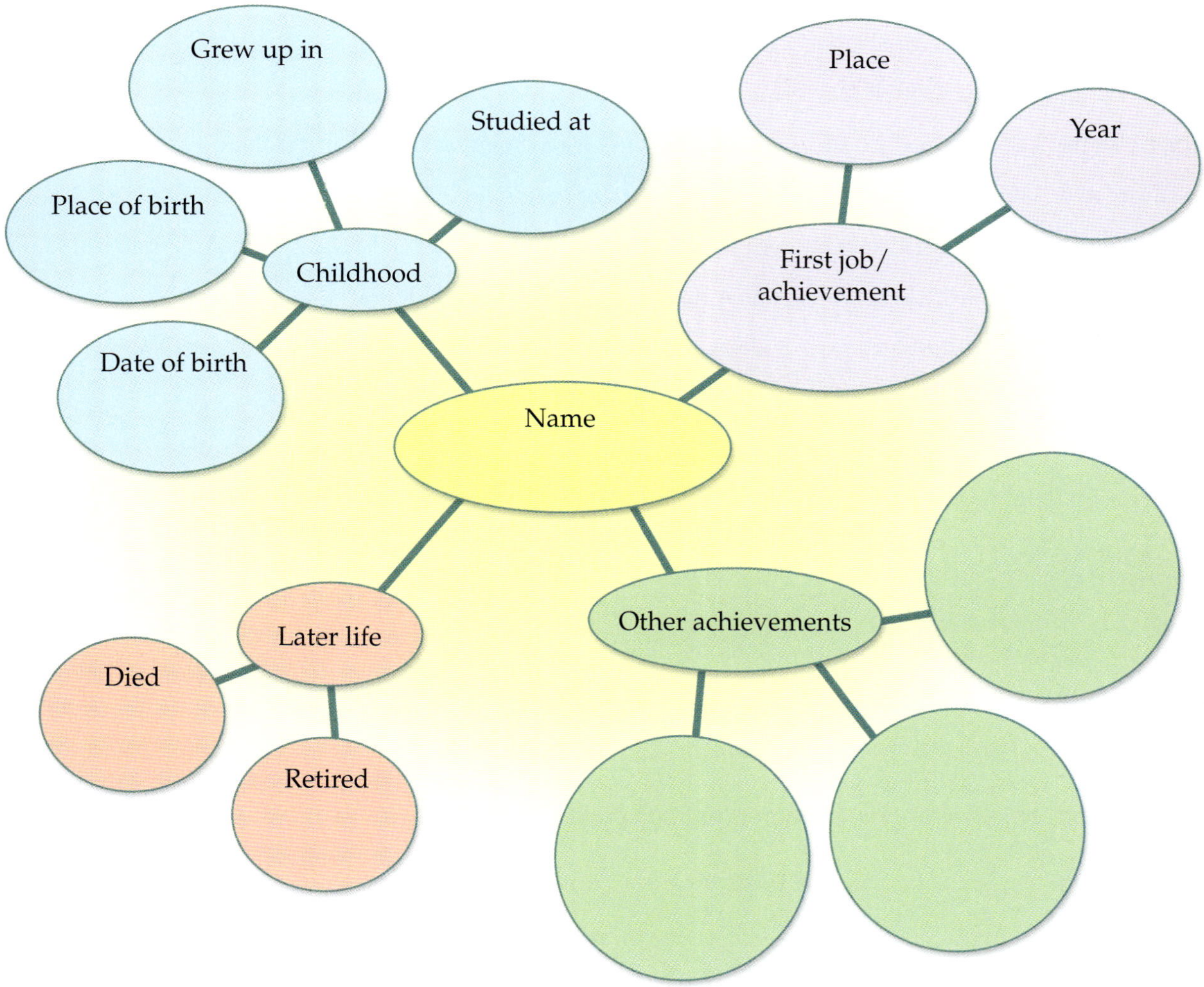

E Write a short biography of the person you chose. Choose one person in the group to write the text. The others help with information, grammar, and spelling.

F Choose one person in the group to read the biography to your classmates.

Reflect...

How did working in a group help you with this project?

Language Wrap-up

1 Vocabulary

Complete these sentences with words or phrases from the box. (10 points)

had	discovered	wrote	built	composed	retired	grew up	explored	got married	graduated

1 Leo Tolstoy was a Russian novelist. He ________________ *War and Peace.*

2 Alexander Fleming was a Scottish bacteriologist. He ________________ penicillin.

3 The actor Tommy Lee Jones ________________ from Harvard University. His roommate was Al Gore.

4 Demi Moore and Ashton Kutcher ________________ in September 2005 in Beverly Hills.

5 Pelé was one of the world's greatest soccer players. He finally ________________ from the game in 1977.

6 Mozart ________________ *Allegro in C* when he was only five years old.

7 Maria Sharapova was born in Russia, but she ________________ in the U.S.

8 Christopher Columbus ________________ the world in the 15th Century.

9 The actor and comedian, Charlie Chaplin, ________________ 10 children.

10 The emperor Shah Jahan ________________ the Taj Mahal in the 17th Century.

8–10 correct: I can talk about life events and historical events.
0–7 correct: Look again at Sections 3 and 8 on pages 110 and 113. **SCORE: /10**

2 Grammar

A Write the correct object pronoun in each blank. (5 points)

1 My girlfriend sent ________________ a postcard from Paris. I was very happy.

2 Joanna and Marcus invited ________________ over for dinner. We were really surprised.

3 George was really excited. The teacher gave ________________ an A on his history paper.

4 Anna's husband gave ________________ a nice gift. She hugged him.

5 Mr. and Mrs. Jones were angry. Somebody called ________________ at 3 a.m.

B Rewrite the sentences in Exercise A as one sentence using a *when* clause. Use a comma if necessary. (5 points)

1 I was very happy ____________________________________ a postcard from Paris.

2 We were really surprised ____________________________________ over for dinner.

3 When George's teacher gave ____________________________________ really excited.

4 When Anna's husband ____________________________________ hugged him.

5 Mr. and Mrs. Jones were angry ____________________________________ at 3 a.m.

8–10 correct: I can use simple past *when* clauses and object pronouns to link ideas in a sentence.
0–7 correct: Look again at Sections 2 and 6 on pages 109 and 112. **SCORE: /10**

In the Near Future

Unit 12

A How much do you plan your life? Check (✓) the statement that describes you.

☐ I plan my life carefully. I don't like surprises!
☐ I plan major things, but not everything.
☐ I don't make many plans. I like surprises!

To do:
go to the bank
buy bread, milk, cheese
make dentist appointment
clean car
write e-mail to Sam
call Mom

B Compare with your classmates. How many people chose each statement?

1 Grammar: present progressive as future

A Language in context **Listen to the conversation below. Circle the time Victor is free to meet his friend.**

Amy: Hi, Victor. It's Amy.
Victor: Oh, hi, Amy.
Amy: Do you have any plans for this evening?
Victor: I'm staying home. I have to study.
Amy: Oh, boring! What about tomorrow afternoon?
Victor: Let's see … No, I'm not doing anything. Why don't we have lunch at Greens?
Amy: OK. Hey, I'm having a party on Friday. Do you want to come?
Victor: Oh, I can't! I'm going out of town on Friday.
Amy: Too bad. Anyway, see you tomorrow afternoon.
Victor: Yeah, sure. See you tomorrow!

Victor is free …

a) this evening. **b)** tomorrow afternoon. **c)** Friday evening.

B Notice **Read Exercise A again. Choose the correct answer.**

1 Victor uses the … to talk about his plans.

a) simple present **b)** present progressive

2 Victor's plans are …

a) definite. **b)** possible.

C Practice **Complete these sentences with the verb in parentheses in the correct form.**

1 I can't see you tomorrow. I ____________ (*go*) to a movie with James.

2 What ____________ you ____________ (*do*) tomorrow night?

3 We ____________ (*visit*) my grandparents this weekend.

4 Lorena and Ali ____________ (*come*) for dinner on Friday.

5 I ____________ (*not do*) anything tomorrow. Do you want to have lunch?

6 ____________ Simon ____________ (*work*) next week?

Watch out!

✓ I'm staying home tonight.
✗ I staying home tonight.
✗ I stay home tonight.

D Now you do it **Check (✓) or complete the activities you are definitely planning for the weekend. Then discuss your plans in pairs.**

- ☐ working
- ☐ going to a movie
- ☐ going out
- ☐ going swimming
- ☐ studying
- ☐ going shopping
- ☐ visiting family
- ☐ other: ____________

A: *What are you doing this weekend?*
B: *Well, on Saturday I'm not working. I'm going to a movie with friends, and then we're going dancing. On Sunday …*

Listening: understanding the main idea p101

2

A Listen to this conversation. Write down any key words you hear that are repeated.

____

____

____

____

____

____

B Look at your list of key words and answer these questions. Then listen again to check.

1 What is the topic of the conversation?
   a) History of the Mayas   **b)** Rick's favorite beaches   **c)** Charlie's vacation plans
2 What is Charlie's main interest?
   a) beaches   **b)** ancient civilizations   **c)** modern cities
3 Does Rick think Charlie's vacation sounds exciting? Why or why not?

C What are your favorite vacation destinations in your country?

A: My favorite place for a vacation is ... because I'm interested in history.
B: Really? I prefer ... because I love nature.

Pronunciation: *–ing* verbs with *–y*

3

A Listen to these words. Notice that there is an extra syllable when *–y* comes after a consonant.

Consonant + *–y* + *–ing*	Vowel + *–y* + *–ing*
worrying	playing
marrying	staying
studying	paying

B Work in pairs. Practice saying these sentences. Listen and check.

1 I'm worrying a lot because I'm playing in the soccer final on Saturday.
2 I'm staying home and studying on Sunday.
3 My sister is marrying her fiancé next Saturday.

4 Vocabulary: phrases with *go*

A Listen and repeat the phrases. Say which of these things you do.

Activities with *go* + gerund

go

swimming running walking bike riding dancing shopping

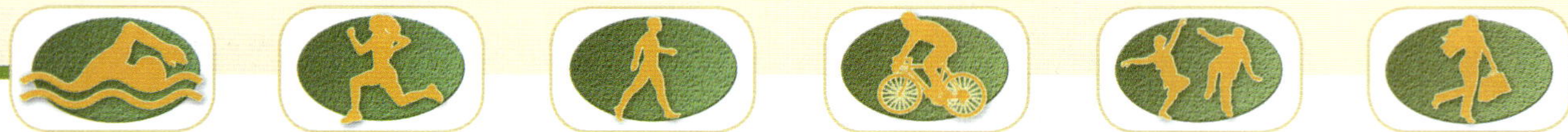

I sometimes go running. I never go swimming.

B Match the phrases to their definitions.

1 go out **a)** to go to a restaurant for a meal
2 go out of town **b)** to leave your house for a social activity
3 go out to eat **c)** to travel to another place, not in your city

C Work in groups. Talk about which of the things in Exercises A and B you are doing in the near future.

A: *I'm going swimming tomorrow.*
B: *Where?*
A: *At my gym.*
C: *How often do you go swimming?*
A: *Three times a week.*

How to say it

every day/Monday
once a day
twice a week
three times a year

5 Grammar: *going to*

A **Language in context** Listen to the conversation below. Why is Giorgio unhappy?

Giorgio: Oh, no! Look at this grade! That's it. I'm going to improve my English!
Tanya: How? What are you going to do?
Giorgio: Well, first, I'm going to study every day.
Tanya: Oh, sure!
Giorgio: I am! And I'm going to get an English-speaking girlfriend.
Tanya: Oh, yeah?
Giorgio: Yeah. And then I'm going to get a summer job in the U.S.
Tanya: Well, I'm not going to worry about my English because I got an A in the course.

B Notice Read the conversation in Exercise A again. Circle the correct option to complete the rule.

We use *going to* for ... **a)** actions in progress at the moment. **b)** future plans and intentions.

***be* + *going to* + verb**	
Affirmative statements	*I'm going to improve my English.*
Negative statements	*We're not going to have a test next week.*
Questions and answers	*Is Victor going to study tomorrow? Yes, he is. / No, he isn't.* *What are you going to do tonight? We're/We aren't (We're not) going to play cards.*

C Practice Look at these pictures. Write about what each person is going to do.

1 ______________________

2 ______________________

3 ______________________

4 ______________________

5 ______________________

6 ______________________

D Now you do it Work in groups. Tell your group about some of your intentions.

A: *I'm going to study harder in math.*
B: *And I'm going to visit my grandparents more often.*
C: *Well, I'm going to travel to a foreign country next year.*

Watch out!

✔ He's going to call me tonight.
✘ He going to call me tonight.

6 **Language use:** reading a post

A Read these posts about people's plans. Work in pairs. Decide which plans sound fun.

> I'm going to volunteer in an animal shelter. I love animals, so I'm really excited!
> Posted by Jenny on August 8

> My girlfriend is having her 21st birthday party on Saturday. 21—I need to get her a great gift! Any ideas?
> Posted by Mack on August 8

> My cousin is visiting and we're going to a family reunion.
> Posted by Gina O on August 9

> Hey, L.A. skaters—we're going to meet at Venice Beach, Sat morning, 11:00. Be there or be square!
> Posted by Hot wheels on August 10

B Write a post about a plan that you have. Compare with your partner.

7 **Vocabulary:** *start/stop* + gerund

A Check (✓) the good habits. Then listen and repeat.

1 ☐ exercising

2 ☐ setting goals

3 ☐ doing all of my homework

4 ☐ eating fast food

5 ☐ worrying

6 ☐ thinking positively

B Complete these sentences with phrases from Exercise A that are true for you.

1 I'm going to start ______________________.
2 I want to start ______________________.
3 I'm going to stop ______________________.
4 Other: ______________________.

C Work in pairs. Read the sentences you wrote in Exercise B. Make appropriate responses to your partner's sentences.

A: *I'm going to stop eating fast food.*
B: *Me, too! And I want to start exercising.*
A: *Good idea.*

Language use: talking about resolutions

8

A Read this article. Answer the questions.

New Year's Around the World

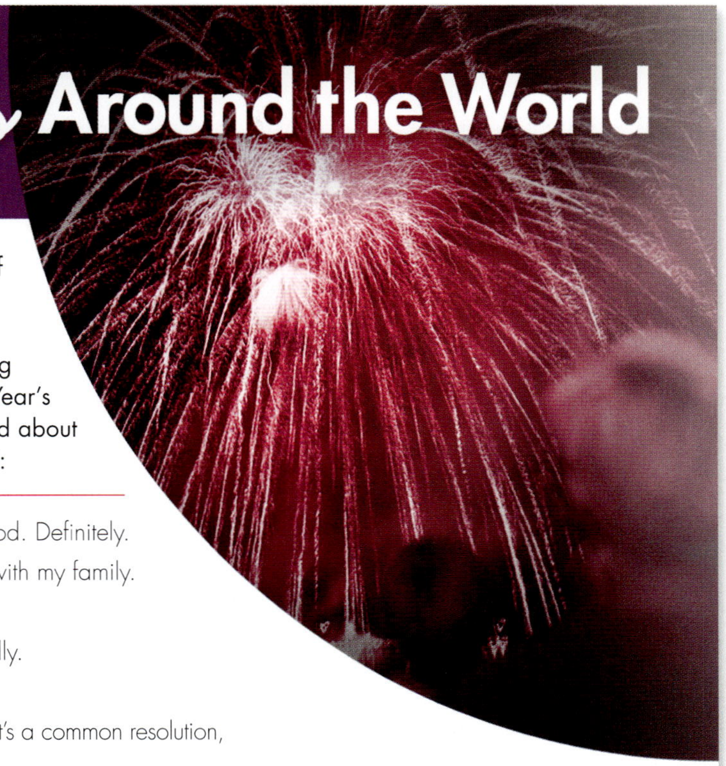

People all over the world celebrate the beginning of a new year. Different cultures celebrate New Year's at different times of the year, depending on their traditional calendar, but a lot of them have one thing in common. In many countries, people make New Year's resolutions. We asked people from around the world about their New Year's resolutions. Here is what they said:

Cathy, Australia:	I'm going to stop eating fast food. Definitely.
Dhom, Thailand:	I'm going to spend more time with my family.
Abdul, Algeria:	I'm going to work harder.
Sigi, Germany:	I'm going to stop smoking, finally.
Alicia, Colombia:	I'm going to lose weight.
Leo, Mexico:	I'm going to start exercising. That's a common resolution, but I'm really going to do it!

1 Do you think resolutions are similar around the world?

2 What are the main things people make New Year's resolutions about?

B What resolutions are you going to make for the next New Year? Walk around and tell your classmates. What are the most common resolutions in your class?

Writing: sequencing and connecting ideas p102

9

Remember that you can use these sequencing words to put your ideas in order: *first, then, next, after that, finally.*

A Most people want to change some things in their lives. Check (✓) five things that you want to do.

☐ exercise	☐ stop eating fast food	☐ do more fun things	☐ study more
☐ organize my time	☐ spend more time with friends	☐ stop smoking	☐ lose weight
☐ think positively	☐ change my appearance	☐ learn to ______________	

B Write the five things in the order that you're going to do them.

C Write about the changes you are going to make. Remember to use sequencing words.

I'm going to make some changes in my life. First, I'm going to make a plan to organize my time. Then, I'm going to ...

lifeSkills

Self-direction and learning: making a learning plan

- Evaluate your strengths and weaknesses.
- Identify ways to improve your weaknesses.
- Set realistic goals.

A **Evaluate your abilities in these areas of English. Use the letters in the key. Which areas need improvement?**

Key:

Excellent = E
Good = G
OK = OK
Needs improvement = NI

Listening:
Speaking:
Reading:
Writing:
Grammar:
Vocabulary:
Pronunciation:

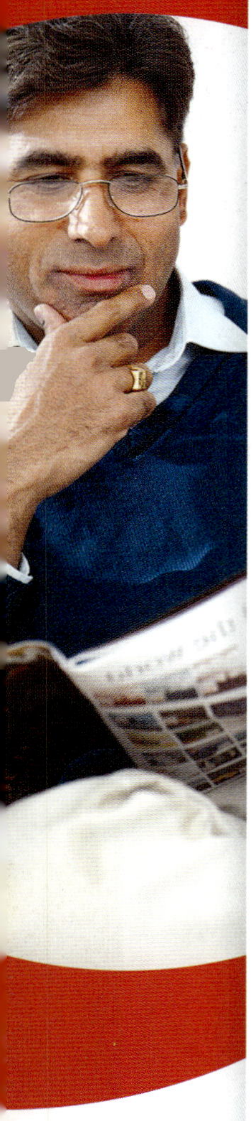

B **Complete the table below to help you identify activities to improve your English.**

- Check (✓) Column 1 for activities that are easy to do in your area.
- Check (✓) Column 2 for activities that you enjoy.
- In Column 3, write the letter of the skill that the activity helps you improve. Write *L* (listening), *S* (speaking), *R* (reading), *W* (writing), *G* (grammar), *V* (vocabulary), *P* (pronunciation).
- Many of the activities give practice in several areas, so Column 3 can have more than one answer.

Things that can help your English	Easy to do in your area?	Enjoyable?	Skill(s) it improves
Reading magazines in English			
Watching DVDs without subtitles			
Watching TV without subtitles			
Talking to people from other countries			
Forming a conversation group			
Traveling to other countries			
Listening to radio stations in English			
Listening to songs in English			
Reading articles in English on the Internet			
Chatting live to international friends			
Writing e-mails in English			

C Work in groups. Compare your answers in Exercise B. If necessary, change your answers.

How to say it

I think ... is easy to do.

Which things are easy in our area?

What do you like doing?

Chatting live can improve your speaking.

D Make an action plan for improving your English. Use ideas from Exercise B or your own ideas. Try to include activities that you enjoy doing and that are easy to do in your area.

Goals for improving my English		
Areas I want to improve	**Things I'm going to do**	**How often**
Listening	*Watch DVDs without subtitles*	*Once a week*

When you make a plan, don't try to plan too much. It's better to start with a few goals and then increase your goals little by little.

E Work in groups. Explain your plan.
Your group can ask questions or make suggestions.

I want to improve my listening and my speaking.
I'm going to watch DVDs without subtitles at least once a week.
I'm also going to ...

How to say it

Are you going to ...?

No, because ..., but I'm going to ...

Why don't you ...?

Yeah, and you can also ...

Reflect...

We often have good intentions, but later we forget about them! How can you ensure that you do at least some of the things on your plan?

Language Wrap-up

p138–139

1 Vocabulary

A Complete these sentences with phrases from the box. (5 points)

running walking bike riding dancing swimming

1 I really should go ______________ more. I never use my bicycle.
2 I want to go ______________ again. There's an amazing pool near my apartment.
3 I'm going ______________ next week. I want to learn samba.
4 I should go ______________ in the park. I just need to buy some sneakers.
5 I want to go ______________ more. There are a lot of nice places to explore near here.

B Complete these sentences with *start* or *stop* and phrases from the box. (5 points)

eating fast food going out exercising doing all of my homework worrying

1 I'm going to ____________________________. I want to improve my grades.
2 I'm going to ____________________________. All these burgers and fries are not good for me.
3 I'm going to ____________________________. There's a really good gym on the next block.
4 I'm going to ____________________________ about the future so much. Life is too short.
5 I really want to ____________________________ with friends more. I stay home too often.

8–10 correct: I can use expressions with *go*, *start*, and *stop* to talk about intentions.
0–7 correct: Look again at Sections 4 and 7 on pages 120 and 122. **SCORE:** /10

2 Grammar

A Use Max's datebook to complete these sentences using the present progressive. (5 points)

1 Max ______________ lunch with Mr. Austin at 12:30 p.m.
2 He and Mr. Austin ______________ the office at 2 p.m.
3 Max ______________ in his office all afternoon.
4 He ______________ Julie for dinner at 7:30 p.m.
5 Max and Julie ______________ dinner at Le Bistro.

12:30–have lunch–Mr. Austin
2:00–visit office with Mr. A.
3:00–6:00–work in office
7:30–meet Julie
8:30–have dinner at Le Bistro

B Complete the conversation between Max and Jim with *going to* and the verb in parentheses. (5 points)

Jim: Hey, I hear you're going to the beach next week. What (1) ______________ you ______________ (*do*) while you're there?

Max: Well, I (2) ______________ (*relax*). I (3) ______________ (*not think*) about work for a week. I (4) ______________ (*read*) a good book, play tennis, and lie on the beach. Julie (5) ______________ (*take*) surfing lessons. She doesn't like too much relaxation.

8–10 correct: I can use the present progressive to talk about the future and *going to* to talk about intentions.
0–7 correct: Look again at Sections 1 and 5 on pages 118 and 120. **SCORE:** /10

Irregular verbs

Base form	Simple Past
be	was/were
become	became
begin	began
break	broke
bring	brought
build	built
buy	bought
catch	caught
choose	chose
come	came
cost	cost
cut	cut
do	did
draw	drew
drink	drank
drive	drove
eat	ate
fall	fell
feed	fed
feel	felt
find	found
fly	flew
get	got
give	gave
go	went
grow	grew
hang	hung
have	had
hear	heard
hit	hit
hold	held
hurt	hurt
keep	kept

Base form	Simple Past
know	knew
leave	left
let	let
lose	lost
make	made
meet	met
pay	paid
put	put
read	read
ride	rode
ring	rang
rise	rose
run	ran
say	said
see	saw
sell	sold
send	sent
set	set
sing	sang
sit	sat
speak	spoke
stand	stood
stick	stuck
take	took
teach	taught
tell	told
think	thought
throw	threw
understand	understood
wake	woke
wear	wore
win	won
write	wrote

Pronunciation symbols

Vowels	
i	**fee**d
ɪ	d**i**d
eɪ	d**a**te, t**a**ble
e	b**e**d, n**e**ck
æ	b**a**d, h**a**nd
ɑ	b**o**x, f**a**ther
ɔ	t**a**ll
oʊ	c**o**mb, p**o**st
ʊ	b**oo**k, g**oo**d
u	b**oo**t, f**oo**d, st**u**dent
ʌ	b**u**t, m**o**ther
ə	banan**a**, comput**er**
ɜ	sh**ir**t, b**ir**thday
aɪ	cr**y**, **eye**
aʊ	ab**ou**t, h**ow**
ɔɪ	b**oy**
ɪr	h**ere**, n**ear**
er	w**ear**
ɑr	guit**ar**, **are**
ɔr	d**oor**, ch**ore**
ʊr	t**our**

Consonants	
p	**p**ark, ha**pp**y
b	**b**ack, ho**bb**y
d	**d**ie
k	**c**ame, **k**itchen, **q**uarter
g	**g**ame, **g**o
ʧ	**ch**icken, wa**tch**
ʤ	**j**acket, oran**g**e
f	**f**ace, **ph**otogra**ph**er
v	**v**acation
θ	**th**ing, ma**th**
ð	**th**en, **th**at
s	**c**ity, **s**ummer
z	plea**s**e, goe**s**
t	**t**ea
ʃ	**sh**e, **sh**op
ʒ	lei**s**ure
h	**h**ot, **wh**o
m	**m**en
n	su**n**, **kn**ow
ŋ	su**ng**, si**ng**er
w	**w**eek, **wh**ite
l	**l**ight, **l**ong
r	**r**ain, w**r**iter
j	**y**es, **u**se, m**u**sic

Communicative Wrap-up

1 What About You?

A Work in pairs. Student A, you want to register with an agency to help you find new friends. Student B, you work at the agency. Interview Student A and complete the form. Then switch roles.

Friends *Express* Agency

Name: ______________________________

M ☐ F ☐

E- mail address:

____

____

Telephone number: ______________________________

Nationality: ______________________________

Date of birth: ______________________________

Occupation: ______________________________

B Work as a class. You are at a Friends Express meeting. You meet each person for two minutes and try to find out as much as you can about him or her. Use these ideas to help you. When you hear the signal, change partners.

NAME?

Occupation?

Family?

Age?

A: Tell me about your family.
B: My brother's name is Julian.
A: What does he do?
B: He's a mechanic.
A: And your parents?
B: Their names are …

Family Act

2

Work in pairs. Look at this famous person's family tree. Ask and answer questions about the people and their connections to each other.

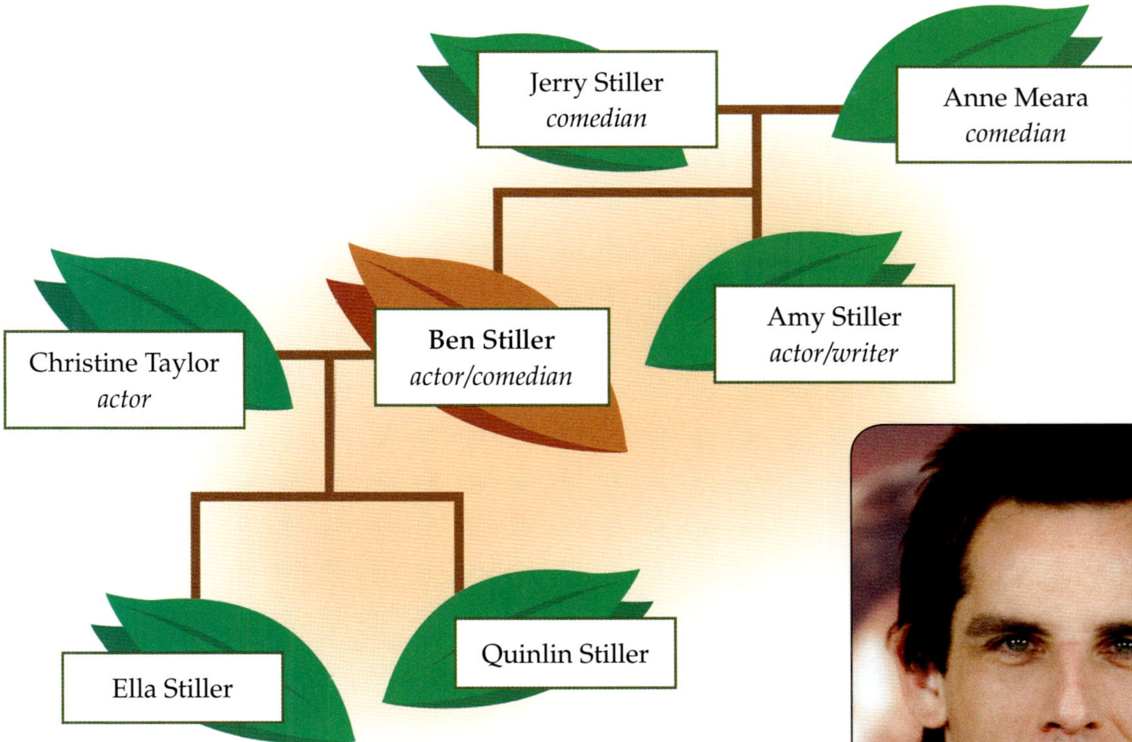

A: *Who is Anne Meara?*
B: *She's Ella Stiller's grandmother.*
A: *What does she do?*
B: *She's a comedian.*

20 Questions

3

Work in pairs. Student A, you are a famous person. You can only say 'yes' or 'no'. Student B, ask questions to find out about the famous person. You can ask up to twenty questions. Then guess who Student A is.

B: *Are you a man?*
A: *No.*
B: *Are you American?*
A: *Yes.*
B: *Are you a writer?*
A: *No.*

B: *Are you a singer?*
A: *Yes.*
B: *Is your sister an actor?*
A: *Yes.*
B: *Are you Beyoncé?*
A: *Yes!*

SCORE YOURSELF!

Score 1–5 for the items below. Score 5 for things that are easy and 1 for things that are difficult.

I can introduce myself.	5	4	3	2	1
I can exchange personal information.	5	4	3	2	1
I can talk about jobs.	5	4	3	2	1
I can talk about family members.	5	4	3	2	1

If you give yourself 1 or 2 for any of the statements, look at the material in Units 1 and 2 again.

Communicative Wrap-up

1 Find Out!

A Work as a class. Find someone who likes each of the free time activities below. Find out how often he or she does that activity.

Find someone who likes...	Name	How often
playing video games		
reading books		
going bowling		
working out		
going to parties		
playing sports		

A: *Do you like playing video games?*
B: *Yes, I do.*

A: *How often do you play them?*
B: *Oh, I rarely play video games. I don't have time.*

B Work in pairs. Tell your partner about any interesting facts that you found out in Exercise A.

A: *Ana likes working out. She works out every day for two hours!*
B: *Really? Helen likes working out but she rarely has time to do it!*

2 It's a Habit!

Work in groups. Take turns rolling a die. When you land on a square, answer the question. The rest of the group can ask more questions if they like. The winner is the first person to reach the end.

A: *On Friday at 7 p.m., I usually watch TV.*
B: *Really? What do you watch?*

START

1 What do you usually do on Friday evenings?

2 What do you do before you go to sleep at night?

3 Name one thing you never do on the weekend.

4 Name one interesting or unusual thing you do during the week.

5 Do you prefer to study in the morning or at night?

6 What is the first thing you do after you get up in the morning?

7 Name one thing you often do on Sundays.

8 Name one thing you rarely have time to do.

9 Do you prefer to do housework on the weekend or during the week?

10 What do you do on Tuesday in the afternoon?

11 Name something you sometimes do with your family.

12 Do you study until you finish or do you stop when you get tired?

FINISH

24 Hours

Work in pairs. Look at this 24-hour clock of one person's typical weekday. Ask your partner about his/her typical weekday and complete the other clock. Compare your clocks. Are your typical weekdays similar?

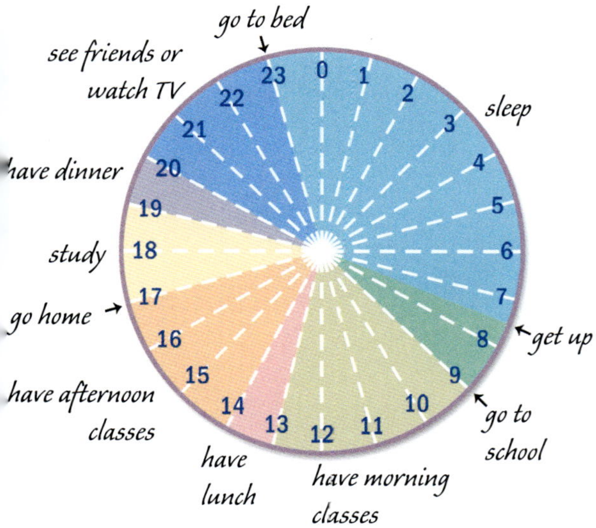

My partner's typical day

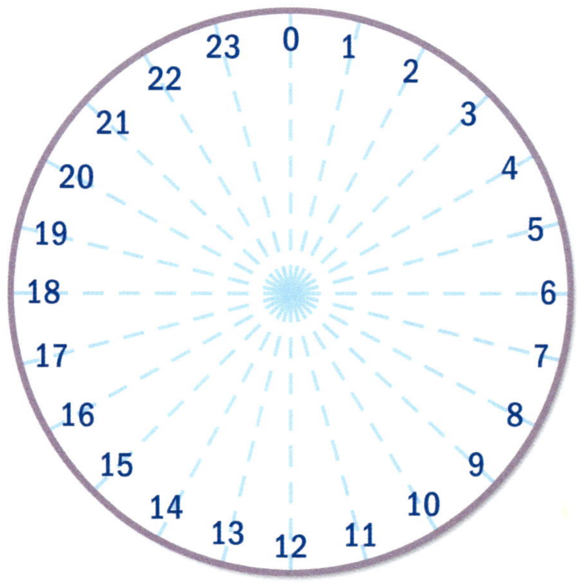

A: *What time do you get up?*
B: *I usually get up at seven thirty. And you?*
A: *I get up at six o'clock on weekdays.*

One Word

Work in pairs. Choose one of the words below to describe each person and explain why.

My best friend | My mom/dad | My brother/sister

- confident
- considerate
- funny
- loyal
- popular
- shy
- sociable

A: *Which word describes your best friend?*
B: *Uh … "funny," because he likes telling jokes. Which word describes your mom?*
A: *Hmm … 'considerate', because …*

SCORE YOURSELF!

Score 1–5 for the items below. Score 5 for things that are easy and 1 for things that are difficult.

I can talk about likes and dislikes.	5	4	3	2	1
I can talk about routines.	5	4	3	2	1
I can talk about when and how often things happen.	5	4	3	2	1
I can talk about what people are like.	5	4	3	2	1

If you give yourself 1 or 2 for any of the statements, look at the material in Units 3 and 4 again.

Communicative Wrap-up

1 Lifestyle Charades

Work in groups. Take turns following the steps below.

- Choose a lifestyle adjective from the box.
- Mime some activities connected to that kind of lifestyle.
- The rest of the group asks and answers questions to guess the kind of lifestyle you are describing.

• relaxing • healthy • boring • stressful • unhealthy • wasteful • green • exciting

A: *Are you writing an e-mail?*
B: *Yes, I am!*
C: *Do you work in an office?*
B: *Yes, I do.*
D: *Do you have a stressful lifestyle?*
B: *Yes!*

2 Guess Where

Work in pairs. Follow the steps below.

- Choose a place that is close to where you are right now. Choose from one of the places below, or use your own ideas.
- Describe how to get there to your partner.
- Your partner guesses the place.

A: *You take the first street on the left. Then take the second right. Go across the bridge and you're there.*
B: *Is it the shopping mall?*
A: *Yes, it is!*

police station
supermarket
café
main square
shopping mall
park
movie theater

3 Help! I Need Some Advice

Work in pairs. Follow the steps below.

- Write down a problem you want advice on or choose one from the suggestions below.
- Swap your problem with your partner.
- Make a list of advice to solve your partner's problem.
- Give your partner the advice.

I don't have any money.	I'd like a healthy lifestyle.
I want more free time.	I can't find a job.
My grades aren't very good.	I need to lose weight.

The Tourist Trail

Work in small groups. Read the rules below.

- Each player puts a marker, such as a coin or an eraser on the "Start of the Tour" square.
- Players take turns rolling a die and moving that number of squares on the board.
- Follow the instructions that appear on the squares.
- When you land on a picture square, say what it is, who you can see and what they are doing there, e.g., for Square 2: *This is a movie theater. There are lots of people. They are watching a movie.*
- The winner is the first person to reach the "End of the Tour!" square.

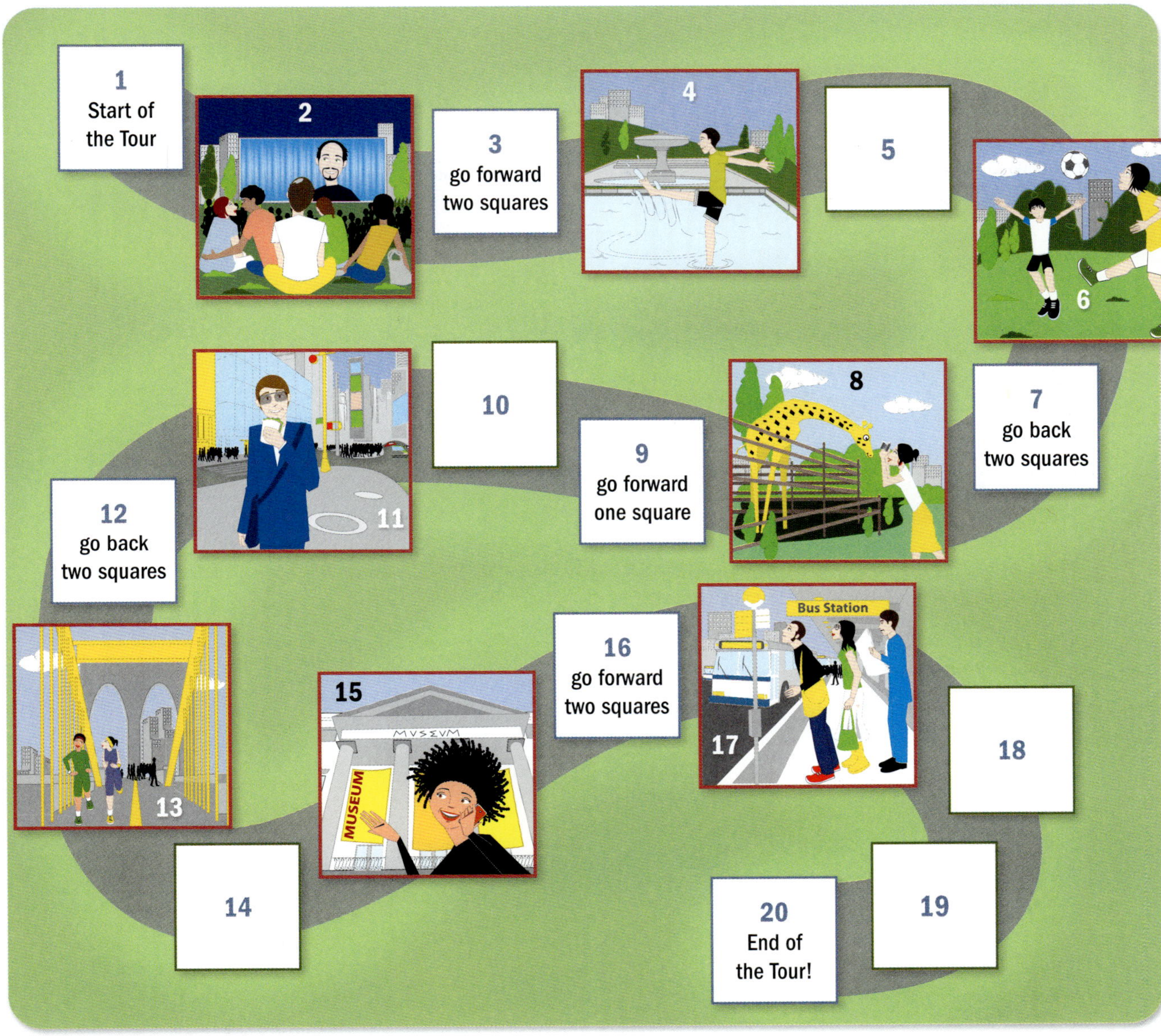

SCORE YOURSELF!

Score 1–5 for the items below. Score 5 for things that are easy and 1 for things that are difficult.

I can ask and answer questions about lifestyles.	5	4	3	2	1
I can talk about places in a city.	5	4	3	2	1
I can give directions.	5	4	3	2	1
I can give advice using *should* and *shouldn't*.	5	4	3	2	1

If you give yourself 1 or 2 for any of the statements, look at the material in Units 5 and 6 again.

Communicative Wrap-up

1 Guess Who

Work in pairs. Take turns choosing a person below. Describe what he or she is wearing and speculate on his or her personality. Your partner guesses the person.

A: *This person looks ... and is wearing ...*
B: *Is it Person 1 ... ?*
A: *That's right!*

1

2

3

4

2 Talent Show

A Work as a class. You are going to find out your classmates' talents and abilities. Ask each student to tell you what they can do well and complete the table.

A: *Jenny, what can you do?*
B: *Well, I'm good at music and I can sing well. I can't act though.*

Name	can/good at

B Work in pairs. Follow the steps below.

- You are going to organize a talent show, based around a theme (e.g. musical show, dance show, comedy show, magic show).
- Look at the things that your classmates are good at.
- Decide what type of talent show to hold.
- Select classmates to be in the show.

A: *Lots of our classmates can dance salsa, so I think we should have a dance show.*
B: *Yes, that's a good idea. Let's choose Ann, Rita, Martha, and Mike. They can all dance salsa.*
A: *And David is good at jazz, so let's choose him, too.*

C Tell the rest of the class about your show.

Guess Who

3

Work in groups of four to play this guessing game. Read the rules below.

- Choose one person in your class that you know well. Compare yourself to him/her for one member of your group to guess. Give your group clues by mentioning things that the person can do.
- If the student who is guessing gets the answer right within three attempts, he or she gains a point.
- If the student who is guessing gets the answer wrong three times, you tell them the answer and gain a point.
- The winner is the person with the most points after five minutes. Good luck!

A: *Andrew, I'm taller than this person.*
B: *Is it Billy?*
A: *No. I can sing, and this person can't.*
B: *Is it Paula?*
A: *No! This person can dance well.*
B: *Is it Georgina?*
A: *Yes, it is.*

The Gadget Review

4

Work in pairs. Read the descriptions of the three people below. Then read the information about the two phones. Choose the best phone for each person.

Jane is 60 and wants to buy her first cell phone. She wants to use it to call her daughter but doesn't want to spend a lot of money.

Mark loves travel with his friends. He wants a phone which he can use to take pictures and videos, as well as check his e-mails.

Alannah travels a lot for work and needs a phone that can help her do work on long trips.

The AP400 Smartphone
Features: Internet, 10 megapixel digital camera, MP3 player, notepad feature
Phone features: caller ID, voice recognition
Weight 100grams
Memory: 2.8 ghz
Price: $500

The L50 Easytalker
Features: large, easy-to-use keypad, text messaging
Weight 200grams
Memory: 1.0 ghz
Price: $75

A: *I think the Easytalker is for …*
B: *Yes, and the AP400 Smartphone is more powerful, so …*

SCORE YOURSELF!

Score 1–5 for the items below. Score 5 for things that are easy and 1 for things that are difficult.

I can talk about clothes and personality.	5	4	3	2	1
I can compare gadgets.	5	4	3	2	1
I can compare people.	5	4	3	2	1
I can talk about talents and abilities.	5	4	3	2	1

If you give yourself 1 or 2 for any of the statements, look at the material in Units 7 and 8 again.

Communicative Wrap-up

1 Make a Menu

A Work in pairs. Make a menu. Put at least two items from each of the categories below on your menu. Include local prices.

Appetizers Soups and salads Main courses Desserts Beverages

B Work with another pair. Tell them what is on your menu. Use your ideas to create a final menu for your group.

A: *You don't have any salads in your "Soups and Salads" sections.*
B: *OK, let's add "Tomato and cucumber salad".*

C Use the menu to role-play ordering a meal. Take turns being the server.

2 Do an Interview

A Think about a place you went to eat recently. Read the questions below and think about your answers.

1 Can you tell me about a place you went to eat recently?
2 Where is it?
3 How was the atmosphere?
4 Was it expensive?
5 What did you order?
6 What did you especially like?
7 What, if anything, did you not like?
8 Do you recommend it?

B Work in pairs. Take turns asking and answering the questions.

3 Find Out!

A Work as a class. Find a person for each of the statements be ow. Write his or her name in the "Name" column. Ask questions to find more information and make a note in the "Notes" column.

Find a person who…	Name	Notes
would like to work in a restaurant.		
is feeling tired right now.		
thinks that cooking is boring.		
needs to study this weekend.		
has to go to work after this class.		
is interested in jazz.		

A: *Alexandra, would you like to work in a restaurant?*
B: *Yes, I would.*
A: *Why?*
B: *Because I love to cook.*

B Work in pairs. Tell your partner what you found out about your classmates.

What's the Story?

4

A Work in pairs. Use the pictures below. Number the pictures in the order you think the events happened. Then write one or two sentences to go with each picture. Include the words in the box.

First	Then	After that	Finally	Last [day]	On [day]

B Tell your story to another pair and see if your stories are the same.

The Last Word

5

Work in groups. Follow the instructions below to play the game.

- Choose one player to answer questions.
- The other players take turns asking questions.
- All the questions must be about the past.
- If you can't think of a question within five seconds when it's your turn, you're "out."
- The last player in the game is the winner.

Player 1: *Did you do your homework last night?*
Interviewee: *Yes, I did.*
Player 2: *What was your homework?*
Interviewee: *English and math.*

Player 3: *What did you do after your homework?*
Interviewee: *I watched TV.*
Player 4: *Uh … did … uh …*
Group: *You're out!*

SCORE YOURSELF!

Score 1–5 for the items below. Score 5 for things that are easy and 1 for things that are difficult.

I can order from a menu.	5	4	3	2	1
I can describe a restaurant.	5	4	3	2	1
I can use connectors to tell an anecdote.	5	4	3	2	1
I can find out about other people's activities and experiences.	5	4	3	2	1

If you give yourself 1 or 2 for any of the statements, look at the material in Units 9 and 10 again.

Communicative Wrap-up

1 Tell Me More!

A Work in pairs. Interview your partner and make notes of the answers.

The Past

1 When and where were you born?

____

2 What was your favorite possession when you were a child?

____

3 Who gave it to you?

____

4 What was your favorite food when you were younger?

____

5 When did you start listening to pop music?

____

6 Who was your favorite group then?

____

The Future

1 What are you doing this weekend?

____

2 Where are you going on your next vacation?

____

3 What are you going to do when this course finishes?

____

4 How are you going to improve your English?

____

5 What are you going to stop doing in the future?

____

6 What are you going to start doing?

____

B Work with another pair. Tell them what you learned about your partner.

This weekend, George is going to a concert with some friends. He's going to see a pop band. He started listening to pop music when he was...

2 Speaking of the Past ...

A Think of something you did that you are not going to do again, or that you are going to do differently next time. Answer the questions.

1 What did you do?

____

2 What went wrong?

____

3 Are you going to do it again? If not, why not? If so, what are you going to do differently?

____

B Work in small groups. Talk about your experiences. Ask for more information when necessary.

Backward and Forward

Work in small groups. Follow the instructions to play "Backward and Forward."

- Roll a die. The person with the highest number starts.
- When it's your turn, roll the die and move the number of spaces indicated.
- Follow the instructions on the square. Answer in complete sentences.
- If you answer the question, stay on your space. If you can't answer the question, move back to the previous space.

SCORE YOURSELF!

Score 1–5 for the items below. Score 5 for things that are easy and 1 for things that are difficult.

I can talk about historical events.	5	4	3	2	1
I can talk about past events using *when*.	5	4	3	2	1
I can talk about plans and scheduled events.	5	4	3	2	1

If you give yourself 1 or 2 for any of the statements, look at the material in Units 11 and 12 again.

Grammar Reference

Unit 1

be—statements

Affirmative	
I am (I'm)	*from New York.*
You are (You're)	
He/She/It is (He's/She's/It's)	
We are (We're)	
They are (They're)	

Negative	
I am not (I'm not)	*from Tokyo.*
You are not (You aren't/You're not)	
He is not (He isn't/He's not)	
We are not (We aren't/We're not)	
They are not (They aren't/They're not)	

be—*yes/no* questions and information questions

Yes/No questions	
Am I	*from Kyoto?*
Are you	
Is he/she/it	
Are we	
Are they	

Information questions (*What, Where, When, How old*)		
Where	*am I*	*from?*
	are you	
	is he/she/it	
	are we	
	are they	

Unit 2

Articles

a/an	We use *a* before singular nouns, e.g., *a singer.* We use *an* before singular nouns that begin with a vowel, e.g., *an artist.*
Plural nouns	Before plural nouns, we don't use *a* or *an*, e.g., *doctors.*

Possessive nouns—*'s* and *s'*

To make a possessive noun…
…add *'s* to singular nouns, e.g., *Brittany's*
…add *s'* to plural nouns, e.g., *sisters'*
Note: *Richard's a car mechanic.* = *Richard is a car mechanic.* *Richard's car is here.* = possessive noun (the car belongs to Richard.)

Unit 3

Simple present—statements and *yes/no* questions

We use the simple present to describe things that are generally true or permanent situations

Affirmative/Negative		
I/You/We/They	*like / don't like*	*music.*
He/She/It	*buys / doesn't buy*	

Yes/No questions		Short answers		
Do I/you/we/they	*like music?*	*Yes,*	*I/you/we/they*	*do.*
		No,		*don't.*
Does he/she/it		*Yes,*	*he/she/it*	*does.*
		No,		*doesn't.*

Spelling: Change *y* to *i* for verbs ending in consonant + *y*, e.g., *He/She studies.*

Simple present—information questions

Question word	Auxiliary	Subject	Verb
What/Where/ When/Why/Who	*do*	*I/you/we/they*	*watch/do/etc. …?*
	does	*he/she/it*	

Unit 4

Frequency adverbs

0% ⟷ 100%

never	*rarely*	*sometimes*	*often*	*usually*	*always*
Note: Frequency adverbs come before the verb *be*, e.g., *Diana is rarely late.* They come after other verbs, e.g., *We often go to the movies.*					

Clauses with *until, before, after*

To talk about the order of events		
before	*I always touch the grass before I start to play.*	We use *before* with the second event.
after	*After I do that, I always play well.*	We use *after* with the first event.
To talk about the duration of events		
until	*I stay in the dressing room until the other players leave.*	We use *until* to talk about an event that continues up to another event or a specific time.
Punctuation: Use a comma if the clause with *until, before,* or *after* comes first. e.g., *I always play well after I do that. After I do that, I always play well.*		

Unit 5

there is/there are with *some, any, several, a lot, many*

Affirmative	*There is a cool festival in my city.* *There are several/some/many/a lot of festivals in my city.*
Negative	*There aren't many/any/a lot of festivals in my city.*
Questions	*Are there many/any/a lot of festivals in your city?*

should

Affirmative	Negative	Information questions
You should go to Harrods.	*You should not/shouldn't visit on Mondays.*	*What should I see in London?*
Note: Don't use *to* after *should*. Don't use *do* with negatives or questions.		
Adverbs of certainty (*definitely, really,* and *probably*) usually come after the modal verb *should* and before *shouldn't* in statements: e.g., *You should probably visit the museum. You probably shouldn't go to the zoo.*		

Unit 6

Present progressive

1 We use the present progressive with situations or events that are happening now or around now.

2 We form the present progressive with *be* + verb *-ing*

3 We don't use the present progressive with some verbs, (e.g., *like, know, want, need*).

Affirmative/Negative		
I	*am/ am not*	*working.*
He/ She/It	*is/ is not*	
You/We/ They	*are/ are not*	

Yes/No questions		Short answers
Am I	*working?*	*Yes, I am./ No, I'm not.*
Is he/she/it		*Yes, he is./ No, he isn't.*
Are you/we/they		*Yes, they are./ No, they aren't.*

Information questions			
Where	*am*	*I*	*working?*
	is	*he she it*	
	are	*you we they*	

Spelling: When the verb ends in *e*, drop the *e* before adding *-ing*, e.g., *take—taking*.
When the verb ends in consonant-vowel-consonant, double the final consonant, e.g., *plan—planning*.

Grammar Reference

Unit 7

can/can't—ability

We use *can* to talk about ability. Questions and negatives do not use the auxiliary *do*.

Affirmative/Negative		
I/You/ He/She/It/ We/They	can	swim.
	can't (cannot)	

Yes/No questions		
Can	I/you/ he/she/it/ we/they	swim?

Short answers		
Yes,	I/you/ he/she/it/ we/they	can.
No,		can't. (cannot)

can/can't with adverbs of manner

1 Adverbs of manner describe an action, e.g., *She can sing beautifully.*

2 Adverbs usually come after the verb, e.g., *She can't dance well.*

Formation of adverbs:

1 We usually form the adverb by adding *-ly* to the adjective, e.g., *slow—slowly, quick—quickly*.

2 For adjectives that end in *-y*, we change the *-y* to *-i* and add *-ly*, e.g., *funny—funnily*.

3 There are some irregular adverbs, e.g., *good—well, fast—fast*.

Unit 8

this, that, these, those

Singular nouns	Plural nouns	Use
this	*these*	to talk about things that are close to the person who is speaking
that	*those*	to talk about things that are not very close to the person who is speaking

Comparative adjectives

One syllable adjectives	Add -*er*, e.g., *old–older, small–smaller.* For adjectives that end consonant-vowel-consonant, double the final consonant and add -*er*, e.g., *thin–thinner, fat–fatter.*
Two syllable adjectives ending in –y	Change the *y* to *i* and add -*er*, e.g., *happy–happier, funny–funnier.*
Adjectives with two or more syllables	Use *more* or *less*, e.g., *interesting–more interesting, popular–more popular.*
Irregular adjectives	*bad–worse, good–better*

We use *less* with all adjectives, e.g., *less cold, less hot, less popular*.

Unit 9

Count and noncount nouns

	Count nouns			Noncount nouns	
	Singular	Plural	Examples		Examples
Affirmative	*I want a banana.*	*I want some bananas.*	*chip–chips* *orange–oranges*	*I want some rice.*	*bread* *beef* *rice*
Negative	*I don't want a banana.*	*I don't want any bananas.*		*I don't want any rice.*	
Questions	*Do you want a banana?*	*Do you want some/ any bananas?*		*Do you want some/ any rice?*	
	Count nouns have singular and plural forms. Use *a/an* before singular count nouns.			Noncount nouns do not have a plural form. Do not use *a/an* before noncount nouns.	

Infinitive phrases

Statements for expressing desire	Questions for inviting
I would like/I'd like to ...	*Would you like to ...?*
I would love/I'd love to ...	*Do you want to ...?*
I want to ...	
Note: Use the infinitive (*to* + base form) after *would like, would love, would have, would need, would want.* To make a suggestion, use *Let's* + base form.	

Unit 10

Simple past—affirmative statements

Regular verbs		Irregular verbs*	
Base form	Simple past form	Base form	Simple past form
answer *carry*	*answered* *carried*	*eat* *go*	*ate* *went*
Spelling: Most verbs: add *-ed*. Verbs ending in *-e*: add *-d* (*prepare–prepared*). Verbs ending in consonant + *-y*: Change *-y* to *-ied* (*study–studied*)			

*See past tense endings of other irregular verbs on page 127.

Simple past—questions and negative statements

	be	Other verbs
Negative statements	*The food wasn't very good.*	*The menu didn't have a very big selection.*
***Yes/No* questions**	*Was it expensive?*	*Did you like Brennan's?*
Short answers	*Yes, it was./No, it wasn't.*	*Yes, I did./No, I didn't.*
Information questions	*How was your weekend?*	*What did you do on the weekend?* *Where did you go?*

Unit 11

Simple past with *when* clauses

The action in the *when* clause happened at the same time or before the other event in the sentence. The *when* clause can come first or second in a sentence. If it is first, we use a comma.

***when* clause**	**Main clause**
When Steve was older,	*he learned to work with crocodiles.* (Use a comma.)
Main clause	***when* clause**
Steve learned to work with crocodiles	*when he was older.* (Don't use a comma.)

Object pronouns

Subject pronouns	*I*	*you*	*he*	*she*	*it*	*we*	*you*	*they*
Object pronouns	*me*	*you*	*him*	*her*	*it*	*us*	*you*	*them*

Unit 12

Present progressive as future

We use the present progressive to talk about definite plans.

Questions	Affirmative	Negative
What are you doing this weekend?	*I'm going shopping.*	*I'm not going anywhere.*

going to

We use *going to* for future plans.

	***be* + *going to* + verb**
Affirmative statements	*I'm going to improve my English.*
Negative statements	*We're not going to have a test next week.*
Questions	*Is Victor going to study tomorrow? Yes, he is./No, he isn't.* *What are you going to do tonight? We're going to play cards.*

Macmillan
Companies and representatives throughout the world

openMind™ Student's Book 1

Language Wrap-ups written by Chris Gough

First published 2010

Concept design and page make-up: Studio Montage
Illustration: Sineval Almeida pp22, 133; Michael Crampton (Meiklejohn Illustration Agency) pp26, 62, 63, 79; Mark Duffin pp8, 27, 52, 58, 120; Abel Ippolito (Beehive Illustration) pp20, 118; Janos Janter (Beehive Illustration) pp38, 46, 86, 88, 91, 129, 135; Javier Joaquin (The Organisation) pp121, 137; Lola & Bek (The July Group) p37; Eva Thimgren (The Organisation) pp56, 110
Cover concept and design: Studio Montage
Cover photos: **Alamy**: Clearviewstock (bl); **Getty Images**: W. Shakell/Life File (tl); Yuri Arcus (tr); IMAGEMORE Co. Ltd (br).
Picture research: Zoe Spilberg
Commissioned photography: Paul Bricknell Photography pp9(c), 9(r), 28, 30(t), 41(b), 43(t), 111, 120, 122(2); Rob Judges p78(b)

Thank you to Mia Caruana, Claire Griffiths, Michael Hickson, Leon Knight, Cassie Odquist, and SAE institute Oxford: www.sae.edu

The authors and publishers would like to thank the following educators and institutions who provided us with invaluable insight and feedback throughout the development of the Mind series:

Carolina Ezeta, Universidad Tecnológica de Querétaro; Karl Schmack, Centro Cultural Costarricense Norteamericano; Maria Elisabeth Schmid de Mattos, ICBEU - São José dos Campos; Martha Patricia Sánchez, Colegio Anahuac Revolución; Leigh Darlaine Langenegger, ICBEU - São José dos Campos; Ricardo Pizelli Goiatá, Curso Bridge over Cam; Franklin Téllez, Centro Cultural Nicaragüense Norteamericano; Jim Nixon, Colegio Cervantes Costa Rica; Rosario Mena, Instituto Cultural Dominico Americano; Leticia de la Peña, Colegio Lincoln; Héctor Sánchez, PROULEX; Eric Tejeda, PROULEX; Arturo Hernández, Instituto Tecnológico de Estudios Superiores de Monterrey, Campus Guadalajara; Grisel del Rosario, Instituto Cultural Dominico Americano; Maria do Socorro Guimarães, IBEU - Rio de Janeiro; Diego Medina, Universidad de Guadalajara, Licenciatura de Idiomas; Julio Prin, Centro Venezolano Americano; María Guadalupe Muñoz, Universidad de Guadalajara, Licenciatura de Idiomas; Lourdes Molleda, Tec Milenio; Frances Gritzewsky, Prepa Tec Eugenio Garza; Magnelli Villanueva Rosales, Universidad Regiomontana; Anderson Lopes Siqueira, ICBEU - São José dos Campos; Emilia Rubenova, Universidad Autónoma de Nuevo León; Lourdes Pérez Valdespino, Universidad Del Valle de México, María Eugenia Rodríguez, Centro Cultural Salvadoreño Americano; Márcia Soares Guimarães, Instituto Cultural Brasil Estados Unidos - Belo Horizonte; Leonor Rosales, Instituto Tecnológico de Estudios Superiores de Monterrey; Martha Larraga, Unitec Escobedo; Cândido Prado, CCBEU – Goiânia; Janet Keyser, Instituto Tecnológico de Estudios Superiores de Monterrey, Campus Cuidad de México; Julie Khatcherian, Manhattan Trade Language Company; Francisco Nieto, Universidad Metropolitana; Artemisa Sangermán, Instituto Tecnológico de Estudios Superiores de Monterrey, Campus Cuidad de México; Nico Wieserma, Instituto Tecnológico de Estudios Superiores de Monterrey, Campus Cuidad de México; Vagner Serafim, Centro Cultural Brasil Estados Unidos; Lourdes Baledón, Universidad Intercontinental; Clara Lucía López, Centro Colombo Americano Manizales; Gabriela Rodríguez, Colegio Oviedo Schontal; Waldo Andrade, CBI Centro Butantã Idiomas – São Paulo; Anthony Shull, Instituto Tecnológico de Estudios Superiores de Monterrey, Campus Estado de México; Tamara Rojas, Escuela Benjamín Franklin; Martha Rosas, Universidad del Valle de México, Campus San Rafael; Fabiano Cella, Universidade de São Paulo, curso Poliglota; Sheila Moreno, Universidad del Valle de México, Campus Tlalpan; Patricia Venegas, Universidad del Valle de México, Campus Lomas Verdes; Luciana Guarnier, Seven Idiomas; Diana Jones, Angloamericano; Carlos Lizárraga, Angloamericano; Emma Domínguez, The Anglo; Luis Cabrera, Universidad Nacional Autónoma de México; Luciane Oliveira, New York School; Cristina Moya, Colegio Morelos; Elda Beraza, Colegio Montes de Oca, Cuernavaca; Elza Massae Sato, FMU, São Paulo; Lucía Canseco Campoy, Instituto Tecnológico de Estudios Superiores de Monterrey, Campus Hermosillo; Emma Luisa Domínguez Instituto Tecnológico de Estudios Superiores de Monterrey, Campus Obregón; Yolanda Domínguez del Instituto Tecnológico de Estudios Superiores de Monterrey, Campus Obregón; Maria Antonieta Gagliardi, Centro Britânico - São Paulo; David Toledo, Universidad Autónoma de Baja California; Alicia Cabrero, Universidad Autónoma San Luis Potosí; Danielle Sales, Senac – Rio de Janeiro; Claudio Barros, Flex Idiomas; Rina de Góngora, del Instituto Guatemalteco Americano; Adriana Alcalá, Kate Cory-Wright, Chris Bauer; Moisés Ramírez; Universidad Chauhtémoc Centro de Lenguas y Linguística Aplicada, Universidad Autonoma de Tamaulipas; Instituto Tecnológico Centro Americano; CELE Mascarones; Ministerio de Educación de El Salvador; Universidad Tecnológica de Nezahualcoyotl; Universidad del Tepeyac; Instituto Politécnico Nacional ESIME CELEX; Instituto Quebec; Colegio La Salle del Pedregal; Universidad Pedagógica Nacional; Universidad de la República Mexicana; Universidad Norteamericana; Fundación Empresarial para el Desarrollo Educativo; Operadora La Salle; Seven São Paulo; Universidad de Oriente; UNIVA; Centro de Capacitación Manuel Sandoval Vallarta; Universidad de El Salvador; Escuela de Jurisprudencia; Universidad de Valle de México, Campus Puebla; Alumni São Paulo; Dr Amany Shawkey, Mrs Heidi Omara, Mrs Hala Fouad (Egypt); Faisal Mreish (Lebanon); Mrs Magda Giomazi (Libya).

Our special thanks go to Louise Fonceca, Jenny Hobein, Bert Vandermark, and our teams of Editors, Designers, Sales and Academic Services at Macmillan Publishers, S.A. de C.V. without whose hard work, professionalism, and talent, this series would not have been possible.

We are grateful for permission to reprint the following copyright material:
p38: Excerpted from The Body Clock Guide to Better Health by Michael Smolensky and Lynne Lamberg. Copyright © 2001 by Michael Smolensky and Lynne Lamberg. Reprinted by permission of Henry Holt and Company, LLC.

The authors and publishers would like to thank the following for permission to reproduce their photographs:
Alamy: Ace Stock p122(tr), APG p71(l), Arco Images GmBH p67(tl), Baby I Got It p85(silver shoes, white dress), Bon Appetit p92(bl), David Cairns p70(l), David Cameron p103(r), Chris Cooper-Smith p40(l), Chris George p77(tl), Jim Goldstein p80(cl), D Hurst p113(t), Iconotec p85(boots), Ilian Studio p7(cr), Ingolf Pompe 25 p92(tr), INSADCO Photography p19(l), Izmostock p80(cr), Niall McDiarmid p85(red dress), Gianni Muratore p67(tr), Mark O'Flaherty p51(r), Rene Paik p80(r), Gabe Palmer p34(cr), Photodisc p85(cream suit), Pick and Mix Images p94(tr), Profimedia p61(bl), ST-Images p77(br), Jack Sullivan p29(br), Henry Westheim p71(t), Peter Widmann p42(t), World Religions Photo Library p49; **Associated Press Images**: p17(br); **Bananastock**: pp7(tr), 14(t), 20(b), 24(mechanic), 30(music), 30(online), 30(friends), 30(gym), 31, 39, 40(D), 40(E), 40(F), 57(tcl), 57(tl), 57(bcl), 57(cr), 64(br), 68(br), 71(b), 72(b), 81, 82, 84(tr), 84(4), 87(br), 88(l), 90(l), 93, 100(b), 102(b), 115, 122(1), 124(r), 124(l), 132(t), 132(b); **Brand X**: pp17(bl), 51(l), 51(c), 54(b), 64(tr), 77(tcr), 85(br), 87(tr), 95, 122(5); **Comstock**: pp77(tcl), 89(t), 117(t), 122(6); **Corbis**: pp 7(br), 12(insert), 13, 23(br), 24(engineer), 27(tl), 27(br), 30(sport), 42(b), 44(t), 54(t), 57(br), 59, 77(tr), 77(bl), 77(bcl), 77(footballs), 84(2), 94(b), 98(tl), 99, 104(l), 114(tr), 117(b), 118(b), 125(t), 134(bc), 135(c), Corbis/ Bettmann p107(Julius Caesar), Corbis Entertainment p129, Gene Blevins p103(l), Jim Craigmyle p9(bl), Cusp p134(br), Edge p135(l), Robert Essel p18(E), Fancy p84(3), Najlah Feanny p14(1), Mitchell Gerber p107(Quintanilla), Tom Grill p69, David P Hall p24(designer), Jon Hicks p104(r), So Hing-Keung p47(l), Image 100 pp32(tr), 57(tcr), 61, Robbie Jack p18(H), Catherine Karnow p18(G), Michael Keller p18(J), Tony Kurdzuk p103(cl), James Lauritz p33, Rob Lewine p58(l), Mango Productions p64(tcl), Lawrence Manning pp15(background), 74(b), Tanned Maury p14(2), Moodboard pp30(movie), 34(cl), Hans Neleman p87(l), Owaki/ Kulla p92(br), Tim Pannell p57(c), Anderson Ross p97(br), Ariel Skelly/ Blend Images pp40(B), 136, Tanner Productions p103(cr), Terra p34(r), Tetra Images p29(bl); **Digital Stock**: pp55, 98(br), 100(t), 105(b); **Digital Vision**: pp88(cl), 88(cr), 88(r), 109(r), 125(b), 138; Fancy/ pp57(bc), 65; **Getty Images**: pp22(br), 27(c), 48(b), 62(b), 68(tr), 72(t), 107(Joyner), 109(l), 123, 134(tr), Gustavo Di Mario p97(c), Sean Gallup p47(c), William King p30(video games), Pascal Le Segretain p17(tc), Thomas Northcut p85(trousers), Punchstock pp18(l), 23(tr), Tom Schierlitz p85(suits), Stockbyte p85(tie); **Grapheast**: p75; **Image 100**: pp24(tr), 43(c), 43(br); **Image Source**: pp14(3), 18(A), 18(B), 21(b), 24(architect), 25(tr), 29(bc), 35(t), 53, 64(bcl), p77(c),77(ccl), 77(cl), 83(r), 90(r), 102(t), 134(bl); **Jupiter Images**: pp50(t), 85(shirt), Asia Images p50(c), Reggie Casagrande p61(cl), Chris Collins p85(men's shoes); **Kobal Collection**: Universal/ Francois Duhamel p108; **Macmillan Publishers Ltd**: Paul Bricknell p77(cr), Haddon Davies p125(c); **Mary Evans Picture Library**: p112, **Masterfile**: p18(C), Steve Craft p18(D); **PA Photos**: pp22(bl), 47(tr), 64(tl), 67(br), 67(c), 105(t), 107(Knievel); **Photoalto**: pp30(TV), 60(tr); **Photodisc**: pp7(background), 24(sales), 34(l), 40(A), 67(bc), 101; **Photolibrary**: p44(br), age fotostock pp58(r), 61(tl), 97(bl), Cultura p41(t), Fancy p135(r), Fresh Food Images p92(tl), fstop p64(bl), Glow Images Inc p57(tr), Goodshoot p64(tcr), Oliver Gutfleisch p74 (tr), Index Stock Imagery p47(b), Japan Travel Bureau p109t), Juniors Bildarchiv p70(r), James Lemass p57(bl), Nonstock p17(cb), Onoky p118(t), Photononstop p97(tl), Radius Imagery p50(b), View Pictures p11(b); **Punchstock**: Digital Vision pp19(r), 30(bowling), Image Source p97(tr), Pixland p44(bl); **Rex Features**: pp68(tl), 110, 114(bl), 114(br), 128(b), 20th Century Fox/ Everett p32(action), Dave Allocca p22(c), Peter Brooker p12, Kristin Callahan p17(tl), Carvalho p17(tr), Everett Collection pp32(comedy), 32(sci-fi), 32(love), 107(Kennedy), Albert Ferreira p29(tc), David Fisher p29(tr), Dan Graves p70(c), Image Source p128(t), Naki/PYMCA p74(tl), Nils Jorgensen p29(tl), Tony Nutley p107(Gandhi), Gregory Pace p21(t), Ponopresse International p107(Pavarotti), Jon Santa Cruz p48(t); **Stockbyte**: pp25(b), 45, 64(bcr), 84(1), 85(handbag), 122(3); **Stockdisc**: pp80(l), 122(4); **Studio 8**: p35(b); **Superstock**: p18(F), Age fotostock p14(4), Francisco Cruz pp40(C), 97(cb); **Ray Tomlinson**: p113(b); **Topfoto**: Ullstein Bild pp68(ct), 114(cb); www.uscampus.com/ p15(r).

CANIEM No. 2275
Series ISBN: 978-607-473-110-1
openMind™ Student's Book 1 ISBN: 978-607-473-111-8

Macmillan Publishers, S.A. de C.V.
Insurgentes Sur 1886
Col. Florida
Delegación Álvaro Obregón
C.P. 01030 México, D.F.
Tel: (55) 5482 2200
Fax: (55) 5482 2203
elt@grupomacmillan.com
A wholly owned subsidiary of Macmillan Publishers Holdings Ltd

www.macmillan.com.mx
www.macmillanenglish.com
www.grupomacmillan.com

Printed and bound in Thailand

This book was printed in October 2009
Thai Watana Panich Press Ltd
Wave Place Building, Unit 3, 9th floor,
Wireless Road, Lumpini, Pathumwan,
Thailand

2014 2013 2012 2011 2010
10 9 8 7 6 5 4 3 2 1